Harry Gruyaert

Introduction by Brice Matthieussent

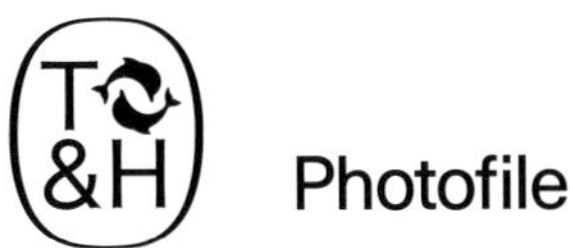

Photofile

The Fiery Pool in the Asphalt

'What, in the end, makes advertisements so superior to criticism? Not what the moving red neon sign says — but the fiery pool reflecting it in the asphalt.'
Walter Benjamin[1]

Harry Gruyaert was born in Antwerp. This is significant. His father, an instructor at the firm of Gevaert, taught him the techniques of photography and filmmaking. Next, after working as a director of photography for Flemish television, he left Belgium and travelled a great deal, to the USA, the UK, France and Morocco. Presenting things in this way, summing up the substance and multicoloured textures of life in quick, broad strokes, may seem obscenely simplistic, but it's nonetheless true, journeys of any kind are important to Harry Gruyaert. And even more so because they mean that he can then return to Belgium. Later. With a different gaze.

For him, the first decisive date was probably 1972, the year in which he created the series of images entitled *TV Shots*. As the terse title indicates, these are photographs of television screens, or fragments of screens, taken during the Munich Olympics, images that combine sporting events, TV shows, news, films, commercials, dog shows, and more. They are a form of photographic channel-hopping, a random sampling of culture, a pot pourri of captured electronic signals whose lurid colours are quite startling. Rather than the subjects, which are often enigmatic, since they are stripped of their narrative context by the taking of the photograph, it is colour and its violent sensuality that are most fascinating to H.G.: the colours of a television set whose aerial has been adjusted by an assistant in order to disrupt 'normal' reception and obtain a striking palette, the colours of Kodachrome film.

Another, more subtle, technical detail is revealed by a second look at these shots: the different screen resolutions and frame rates used in the various countries where the *TV Shots* were taken. These could be used to create comparisons between the two forms of analogue TV technology, establishing a kind of typology that runs through this series of ostensibly fleeting images; this is not the kind of graphic archaeology of industrial buildings in black and white that was practised shortly afterwards by Bernd and Hilla Becher, but the zeitgeist is nonetheless palpable in this set of works. All the more so since at around the same time, a similar exploration of electronic distortions was being carried out by Nam June Paik, in installations that owe nothing to photography but are instead closer to sculptures.

In addition, the bright, chemical, saturated, strident, psychedelic, clashing colour schemes recall Pop art, and more specifically Warhol's screenprints, such as the flat two-dimensional *Flowers* series of the mid-1960s. Although flatscreens did not yet exist in 1972, the glass surface of a TV set was probably one of the objects with the least depth of field that a photographer could find. It was also a frame, and a ready-made image. In addition, even the planned viewing of a TV programme reflects the way in which Marcel Duchamp viewed the creation of his own ready-mades: Duchamp saw himself as having an 'appointment' with a ready-made 'at a set time', just as H.G. might have waited for the broadcast of a particular show in order to capture a prefabricated image for inclusion in his *TV Shots*.

A close relation of the TV screen is the shop window. Shop windows are significant in the history of photography: they appear in images by Eugène Atget, Walker Evans, the Surrealists in general, Lee Friedlander of course, Stephen Shore (the window full of electric light bulbs, lit by the sun), and H.G. himself. A TV screen is a shop window plus electricity. Both are glass interfaces between spaces that are physically separated but visually juxtaposed. Cropping, clarity,

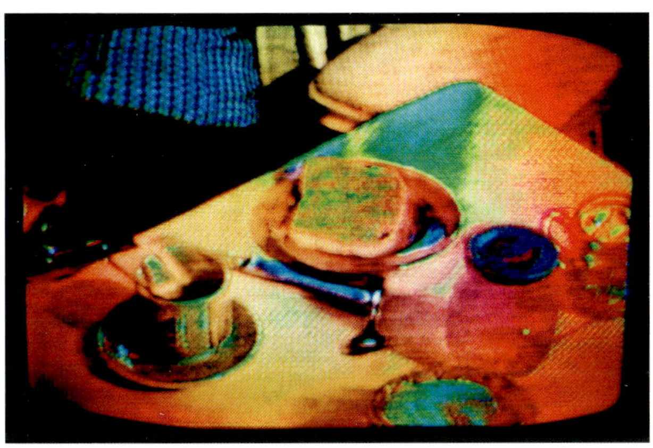

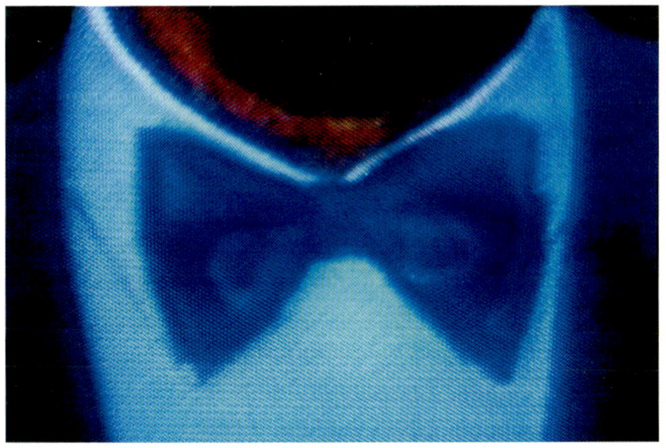

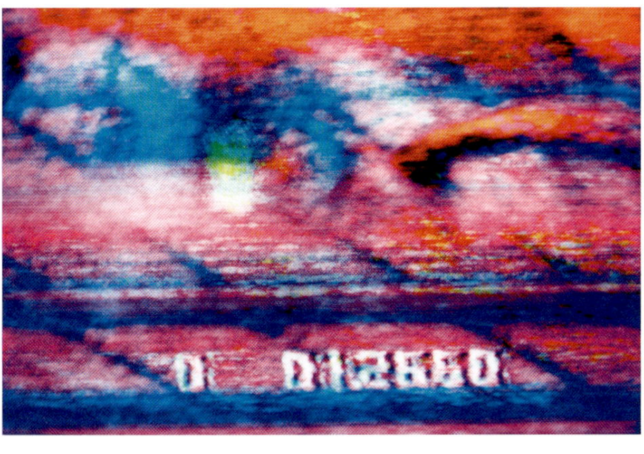

frontality: the modern photographic act owes a great deal to the confrontation between a photographer and a shop window. Before becoming Andy Warhol, Andrew Warhola had a successful career as a window-dresser for New York department stores.

The year 1972 saw the opening of the exhibition *American Surfaces*, by Stephen Shore, at the Light Gallery in New York: 320 colour prints which were bought up by the Metropolitan Museum of Art. Four years later, in 1976, John Szarkowski, head of the photography department at MoMA in New York, curated an exhibition by a virtual unknown, William Eggleston, and published the book *William Eggleston's Guide*. Thus, within the space of four years, American museums began to welcome colour photography, which had been formerly viewed with disdain by the art world. This is not the place to go into the relationships of scorn, envy or indifference that exist between photographers and the art world, now more than ever. The significant thing is that H.G. saw the William Eggleston exhibition in New York and it made an impact on him.

I think Szarkowski offers a good explanation for this impact in his foreword to the book *William Eggleston's Guide*: with only a few exceptions, including Stephen Shore, colour photography had until this point tended to lead to two categories of failure. 'The more interesting of these', wrote Szarkowski, 'might be described as black-and-white photographs made with colour film, in which the problem of colour is solved by inattention. The better photographs of the old *National Geographic* were often of this sort: no matter how cobalt the blue skies and how crimson the red shirts, the colour in such pictures is extraneous – a failure of form. Nevertheless such pictures are often interesting, even if shapeless and extravagant, in the same way that casual conversation is often interesting. The second category of failure in colour photography comprises photographs of beautiful colours in pleasing relationships. The nominal subject matter of these pictures is often the walls of old buildings, or the prows of sailboats reflected in rippled water. Such photographs can be recognized by their resemblance to reproductions of Synthetic Cubist or Abstract Expressionist paintings. It is their unhappy fate to remind us of something similar but better.'[2]

On one hand, the failure of form, inattention and avoidance
of the problem; on the other hand, the prettiness of a form of
pictorialism that was both revamped and outdated. In this light,
we can better understand the reactions of Walker Evans or Henri
Cartier-Bresson, who both considered colour photography to be
'vulgar'; rather than being closed to this new concept out of principle,
they formed their judgment based on the work they saw, and they
were right. At least at the time, which was before the mid-1970s.

Szarkowski wrote that for the first time in Eggleston's
photographs, the sky and the colour blue were no longer two
separate things: it was not possible to say 'the sky is blue', grammar
was misleading, because the two concepts 'sky' and 'blue' were
perceived by our senses at the same time, in that pre-linguistic
unity of perception that Yves Klein surely wanted us to rediscover
through his monochrome paintings. The blue and the sky are one
thing: Szarkowski concludes that Eggleston's images – and those
of H.G. – 'are not photographs of colour, any more than they are
photographs of shapes, textures, objects, symbols, or events, but
rather photographs of experience, as it has been ordered and
clarified within the structures imposed by the camera.'[3]

In other words, as H.G. himself said, 'Colour is a means
of sculpting what I see. Colour does not illustrate a subject or
the scene that I am photographing, it's a value in itself. It's the
emotion of photography.' It is interesting that H.G. compares
his photographic practice to sculpture, rather than to painting.
In the early 1950s, Matisse created a wealth of cut-out collages
from painted paper, including the *Jazz* series, and said: 'Cutting
directly into colour reminds me of the way sculptors directly
shape their material' and 'Drawing with scissors on sheets of pre-
painted paper, using the same gesture to connect line and colour,
contour and surface.'[4] The significant thing was that it was this
single gesture that made form, content and colour melt together
into a single image in which 'line and colour, contour and surface'
were inextricably merged.

Such was the impact created by Eggleston in 1976 and felt by
H.G. Both were from the same generation and they shared the same

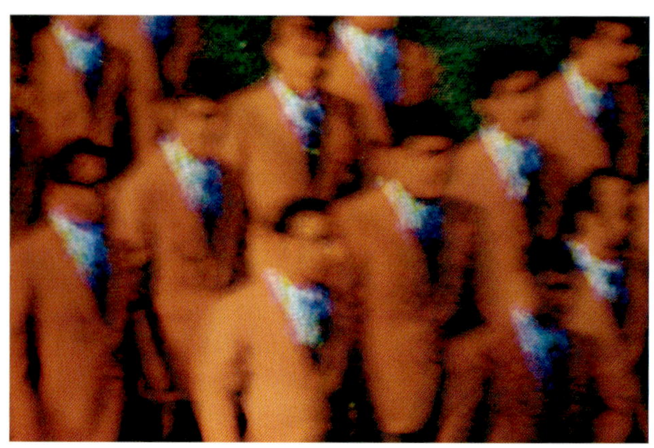

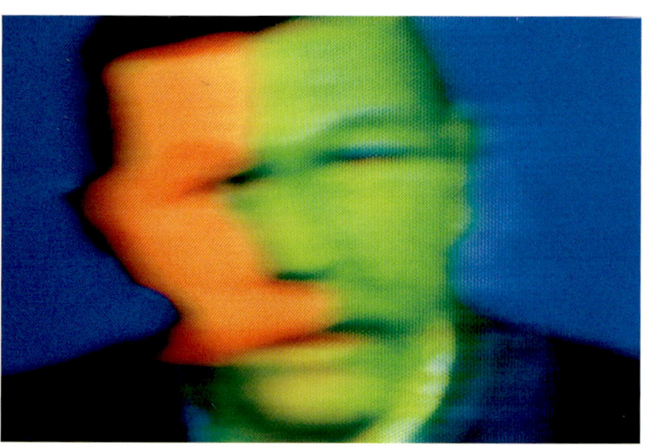

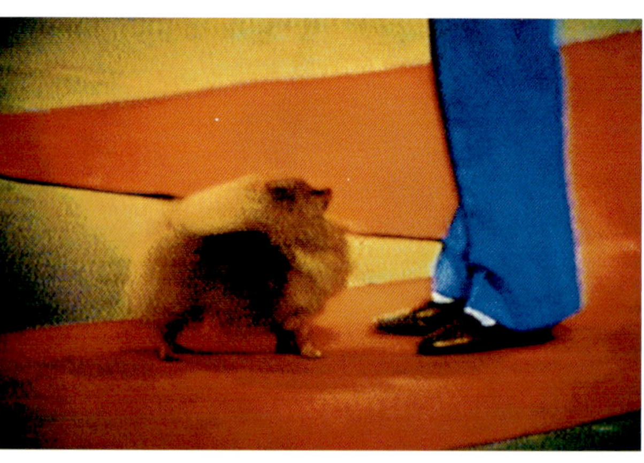

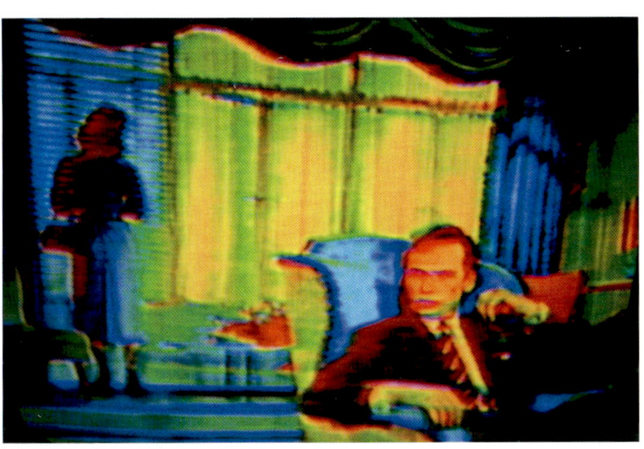

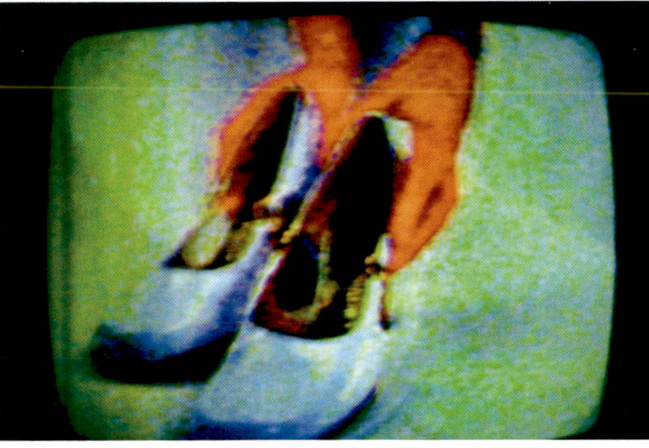

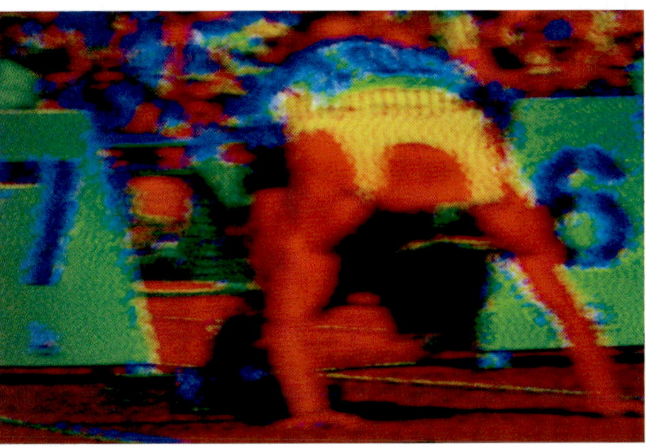

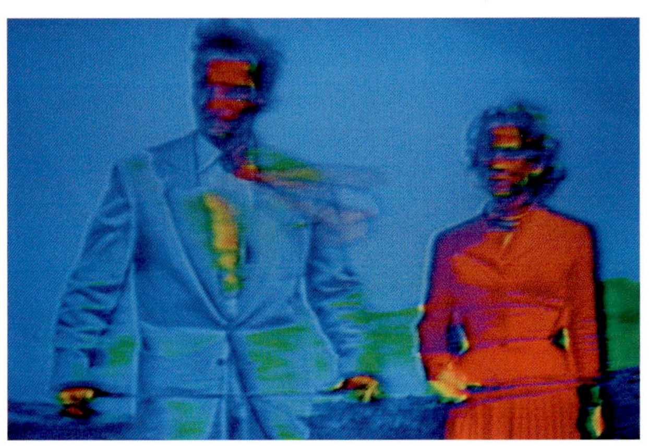
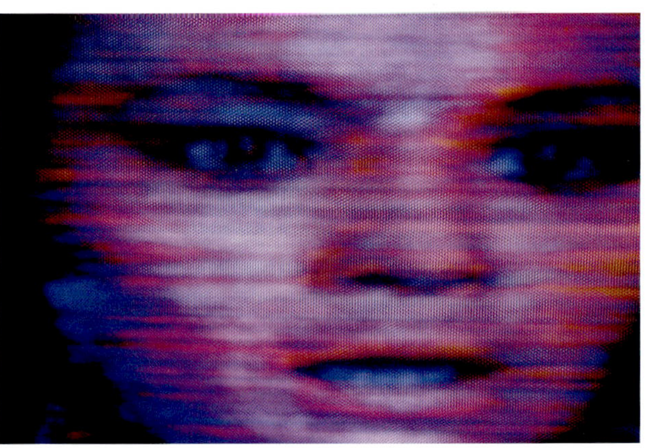
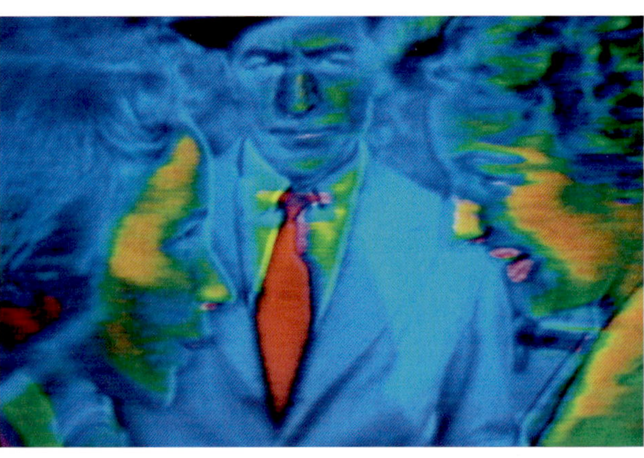

visual references for colour: modern painting, magazines, television, cinema. But in every other way, they were different: Eggleston's best photographs were taken in a relatively small area of Mississippi, while H.G.'s came from all over the world; Eggleston composed his images with a radiating centrality, while H.G. deliberately reverses the respective importance of the centre and the periphery; ultimately, what has been called the 'flux of consciousness' in Eggleston's work or that of Stephen Shore, their unique way of turning a published series of images into a sort of personal diary or covert self-portrait, is very different from the approach taken by H.G., to whom every image is an autonomous whole, a world in itself.

Let's go back. First, to a land expanded to the size of the world. Morocco was a decisive encounter in itself. For twenty years, H.G. criss-crossed this country, every trip allowing him to discover and rediscover 'a splendid harmony between forms, colours, everyday gestures and nature'. The light of Morocco, simultaneously harsh and gentle, blinding and motherly, abstract and sensual, gave rise, in my opinion, to two kinds of images from H.G. Those of the first category are violent urban oppositions between light and shade, large areas of flat black that cut through walls of glowing ochre and recall the monumental presence of Richard Serra's metal sculptures. A cyclist passes by, a shadow among shadows; a standing man turns his back on us, minuscule and perfectly positioned close to the corner of a yellow building. The decisive moment lurks in wait. H.G. has always admired Henri Cartier-Bresson, and the 'effacement' that allowed him to get up close to people without disturbing them. But in the case of H.G.'s work, perhaps it would be more appropriate to speak of the 'decisive light'. Or better yet, a decisive encounter with colour and light.

The second type of Moroccan image could be called by a name provocatively borrowed from a painting by Matisse, 'ornamental figures on a decorative ground': bodies wrapped in colourful floral

Opposite and previous pages:
Images from the series *TV Shots*, 1972.

or striped robes, bodies that are faceless and therefore sculptural, carved out of colour, against a background of gaudy tents or roughly plastered walls, resembling those of India. A woman lifts a scarf to cover her face and shows us the unexpected gift of a baby sleeping on her back, wrapped in a striped red and white blanket. Once again, the decisive moment is close at hand, even though this revelatory modesty and the perfect positioning of the goat in the confined space recall a theatrical performance or film scene.

All of these images are clearly a thousand miles away from cheap exoticism and chintzy quaintness. They are also a long way from reportage photography, a genre that H.G. has great respect for, but whose objectives he does not share. At this point, it is interesting to look at the concept of shock. Not in the horrifying sense, but as a way of describing the sudden burst of emotion created by an encounter – whether with the images of another photographer, a country, a work of art, or the premonition of a potential image. Shock, in H.G.'s terms, is the chance to capture a complex encounter with colour and light. Walter Benjamin was the first to identify shock as a principle for aesthetically perceiving the modern city: the shock of signposts, the shock of advertising, the shock of speed. In *One-Way Street* (1928), Benjamin wrote: '[The advertisement] abolishes the space where contemplation moved and all but hits us between the eyes with things as a car, growing to gigantic proportions, careens at us out of a film screen.'[5] Shock is what keeps us glued to our seat at the cinema and what makes us see the city as a violent series of cinematic images. H.G.'s photographs not only bear witness to this kind of shock, but in turn create within the viewer a wave of sensuality and violence, a troubling, unsettling disruption, the sudden intrusion of extreme strangeness, a kind of amazement that redoubles the amazement created by any kind of photography.

After Morocco and then India, he found it necessary to return to Belgium. This is significant because H.G. wanted to look more closely into his Flemish heritage: the images he created, along with many others, show the clear influence of Belgian surrealism: unexpected, even incongruous encounters, not between an umbrella and a sewing machine on a dissecting table, as Lautréamont described, but between

a man and a woman gazing at a Magritte painting in a museum, or
perhaps between a parade of soldiers in Napoleonic uniform and
a yellow car, parked in a modern side street as if waiting in ambush.
There is wit there, and an element of uncertainty, the humour
of objective chance, the playfulness of the unexpected, a sort of
'metaphysical photography' that can also be found in the images
of deserted streets or empty public spaces, criss-crossed with huge
shadows or punctuated with solitary signposts.

Let's go back. 'Reality', H.G. said, 'is like a collage by Picasso
whose elements were not meant to be combined, but which, when
suddenly juxtaposed, mean and say something that's original
and very powerful, which could not be grasped before.' A collage
of disparate elements, or perhaps a cinematic montage whose
overall meaning exceeds the individual significance of the shots
from which it has been made… An assemblage that is often off-
centre, or perhaps a scattering of zones of visual stimulation, if not
a central void, or better still a swarm of micro-events, a kind of
chaos, an accumulation of signs, in Japan, Las Vegas, Egypt. Unlike
Eggleston's images, but rather closer to the urban landscapes of
Friedlander, H.G.'s photographs shun the dogma of centrality, the
rules of construction that have survived since the Renaissance; they
telescope together different spaces and forms of light – artificial and
natural; they are fixated on borders, interfaces, margins, things that
are happening in the periphery, not in order to bolster the centre and
reaffirm its primacy right up to the edges but in order to create other
relationships, deploy lines of force, remove hierarchies, widen the
visual field, give equal weight to all areas within an image, somehow
'flattening' it to reveal its sensual, teeming splendour without ever
giving in to the abstract tyranny of the Whole.

Nowhere here do we see the overarching idea of an intimate
diary, or even a chronicle. Is this effacement of the artist similar
to the 'furtiveness' of Cartier-Bresson? Does the disappearance
of human figures from these images or at least their reduction in
size and virtual absence of faces indicate a similar disappearance
of the artist behind the work? I don't believe so. Although these
images are situated at the opposite end of the scale from the kind

of humanist photography whose foundations seem to crumble a little more every day, they spin a thread that eventually forms the outlines of a self-portrait: an image of a sentimental traveller, an unrepentant *flâneur* and even occasional predator, whose creations, simultaneously prosaic and poetic, violent and subtle, and always boldly contemporary, once again transfigure the banal and reveal the face of art and life to us.

Brice Matthieussent

Notes

1   Walter Benjamin, 'This Space for Rent', in *One-Way Street* (1928), London: New Left Books, 1979.

2   *William Eggleston's Guide*, New York: MoMA, 1976.

3   *William Eggleston's Guide*, New York: MoMA, 1976.

4   Henri Matisse, *Jazz*, Paris: Éditions Verve, 1947.

5   Walter Benjamin, 'This Space for Rent', in *One-Way Street* (1928).

1. La Courneuve, France, 1985.

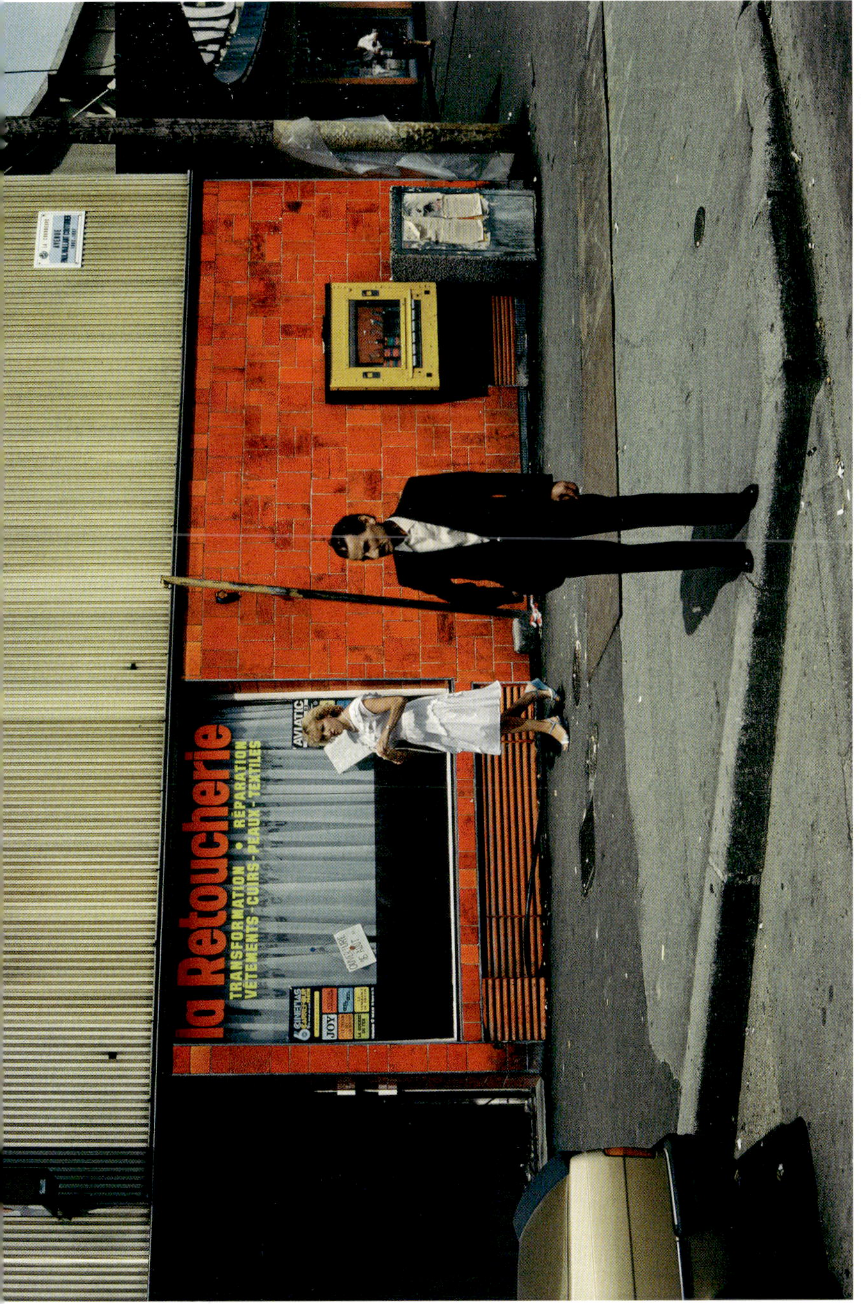

la Retoucherie
TRANSFORMATION • RÉPARATION
VÊTEMENTS - CUIRS - PEAUX - TEXTILES
AVIATIC

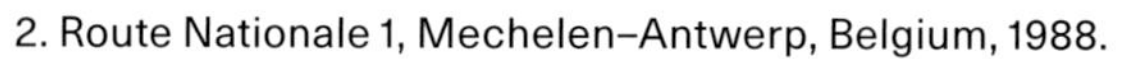

2. Route Nationale 1, Mechelen–Antwerp, Belgium, 1988.

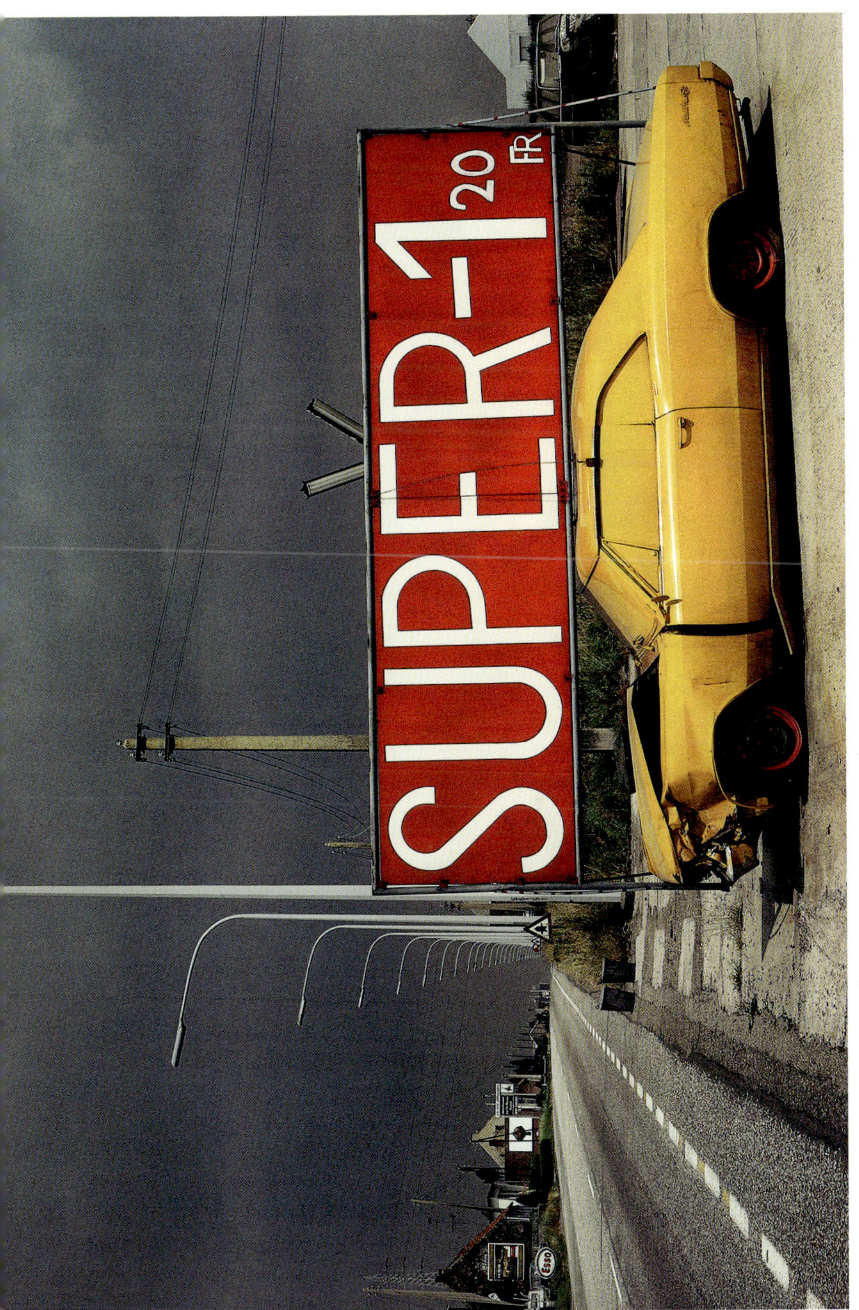

SUPER-1.20 FR

3. County Kerry, Ireland, 1983.

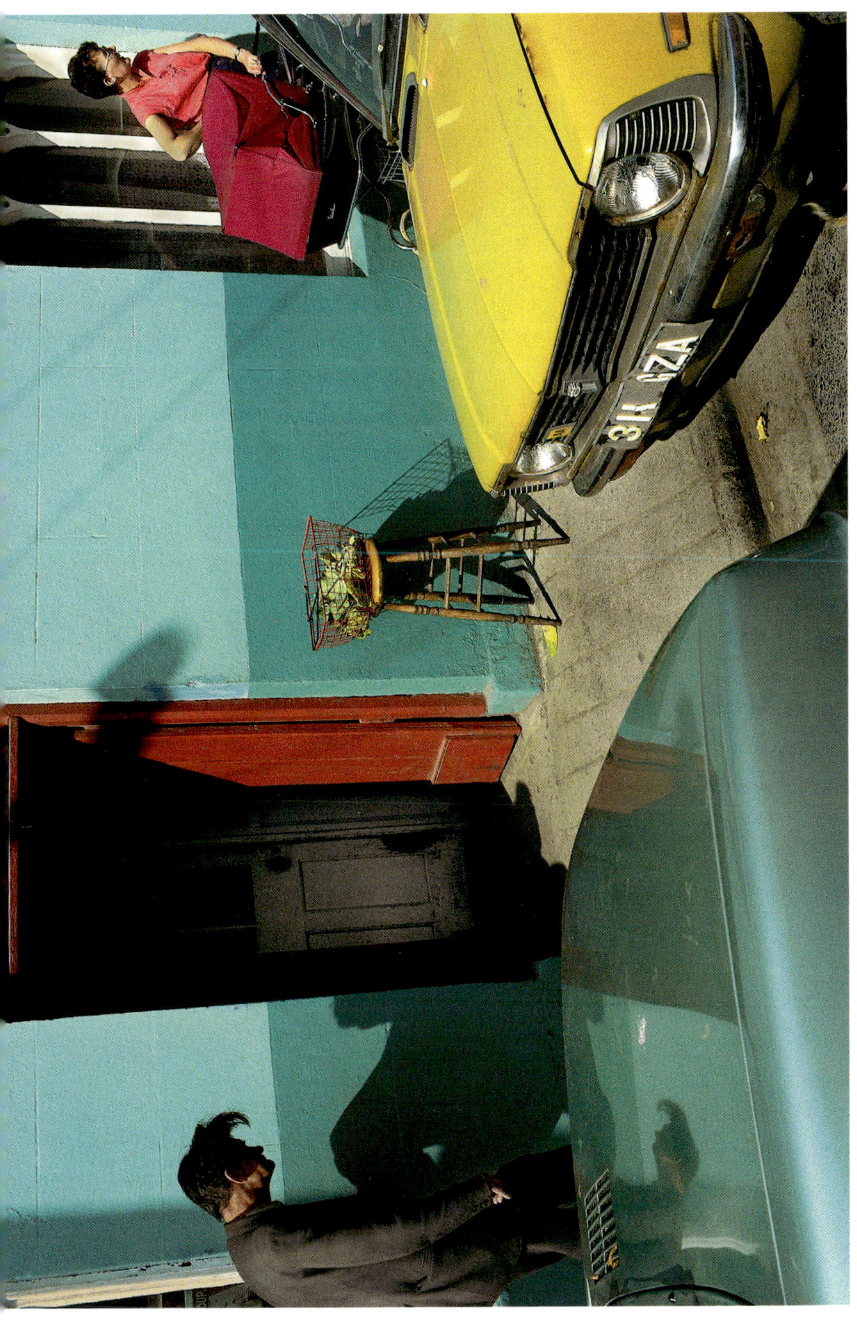

4. Rue Royale, Brussels, 1981.

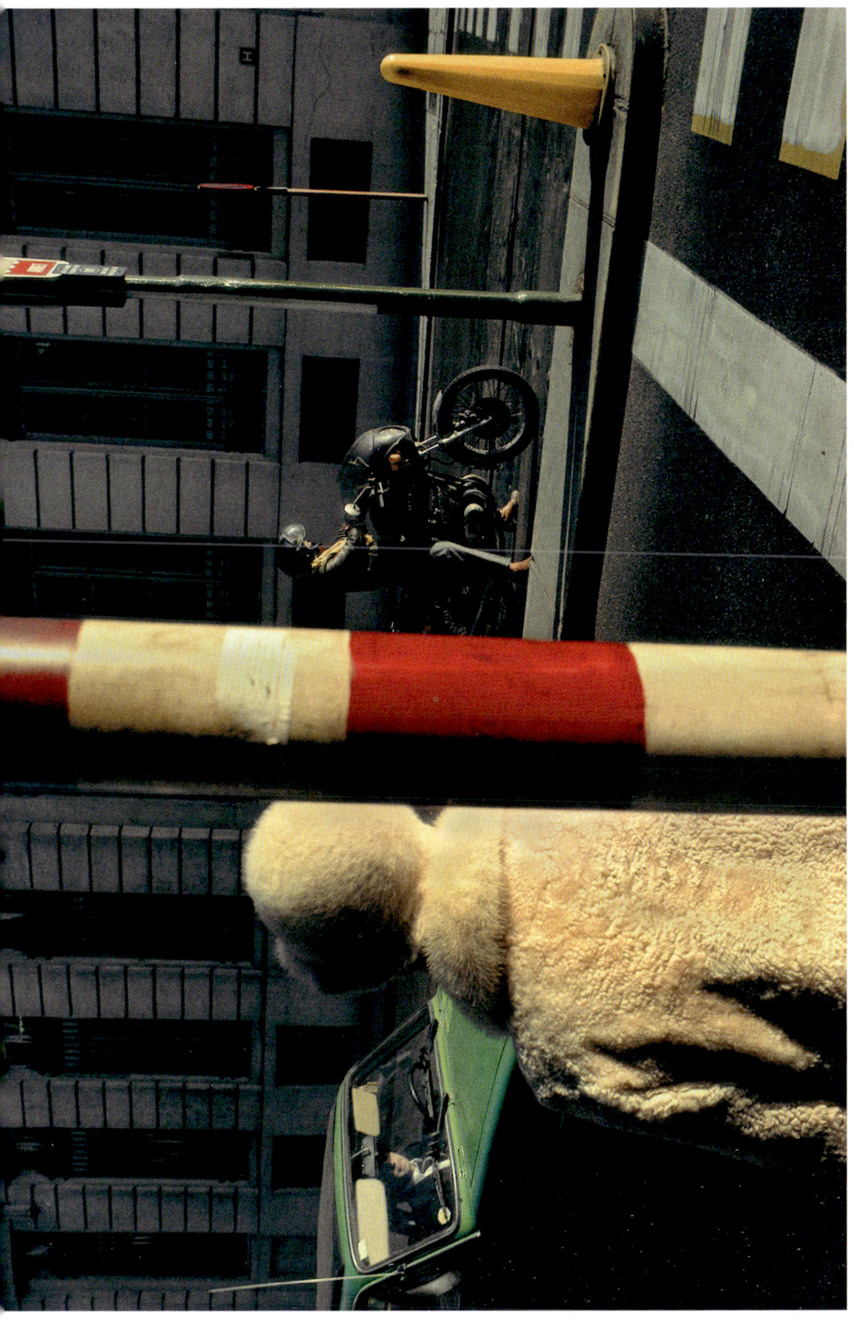

5. Commemoration of the Battle of Waterloo, Waterloo, Belgium, 1981.

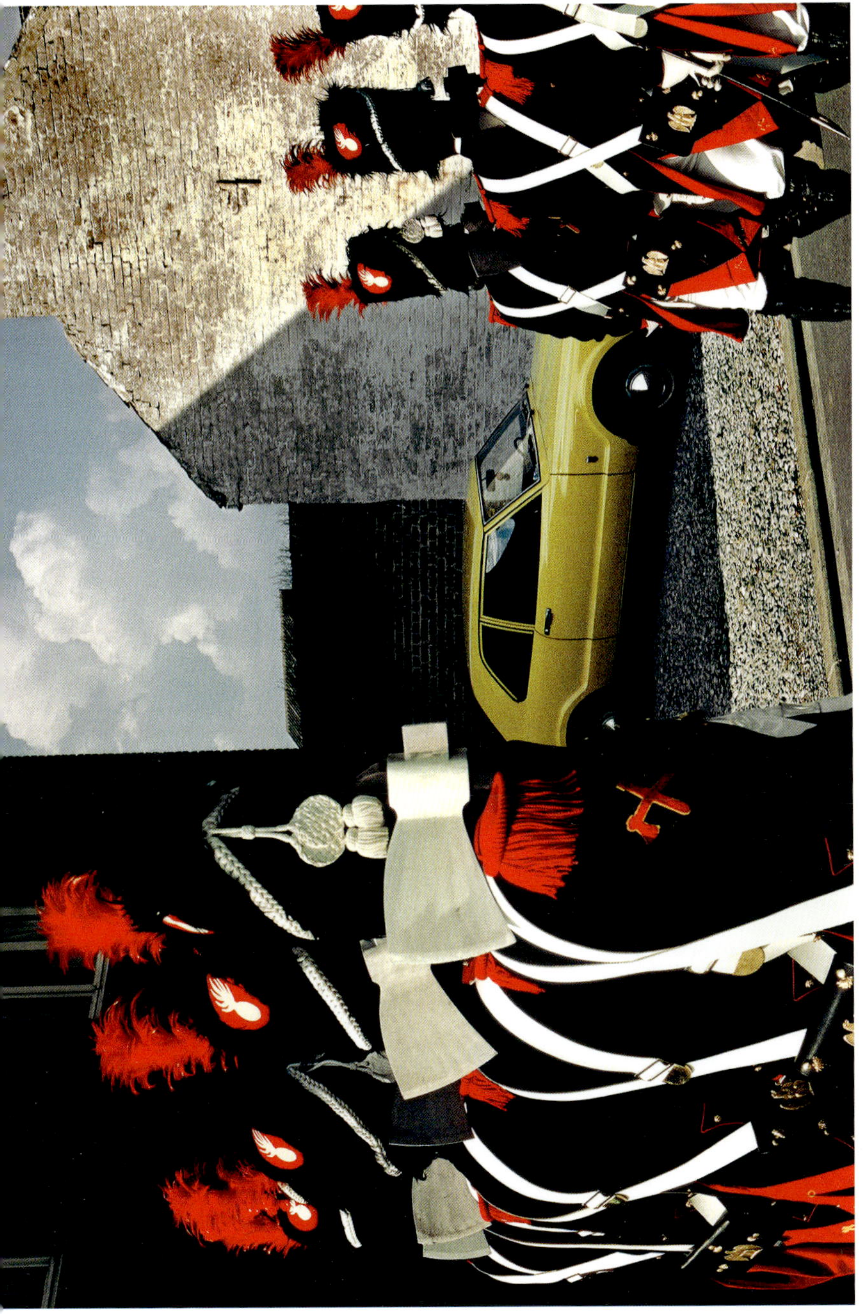

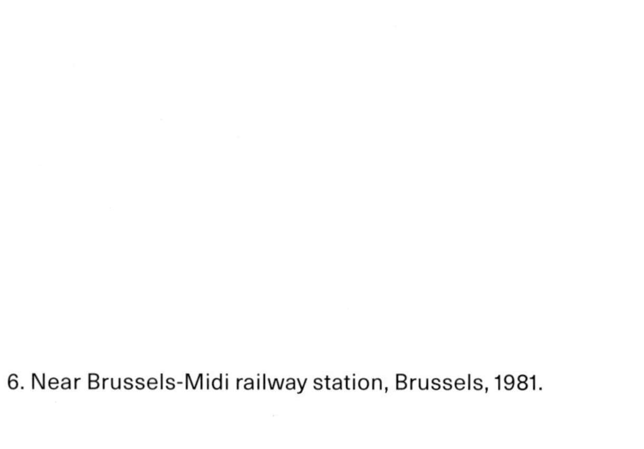

6. Near Brussels-Midi railway station, Brussels, 1981.

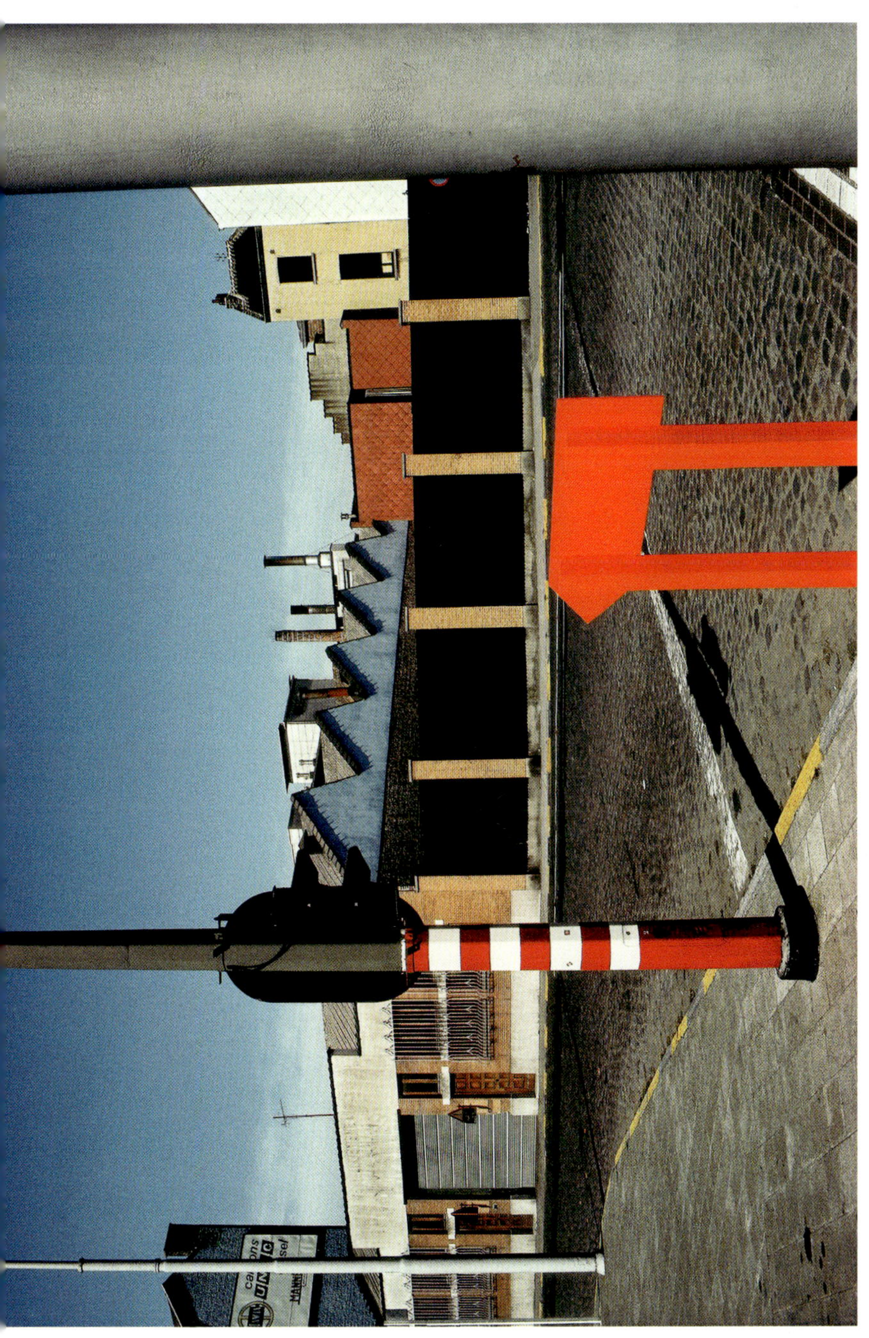

7. Antwerp, Belgium, 1988.

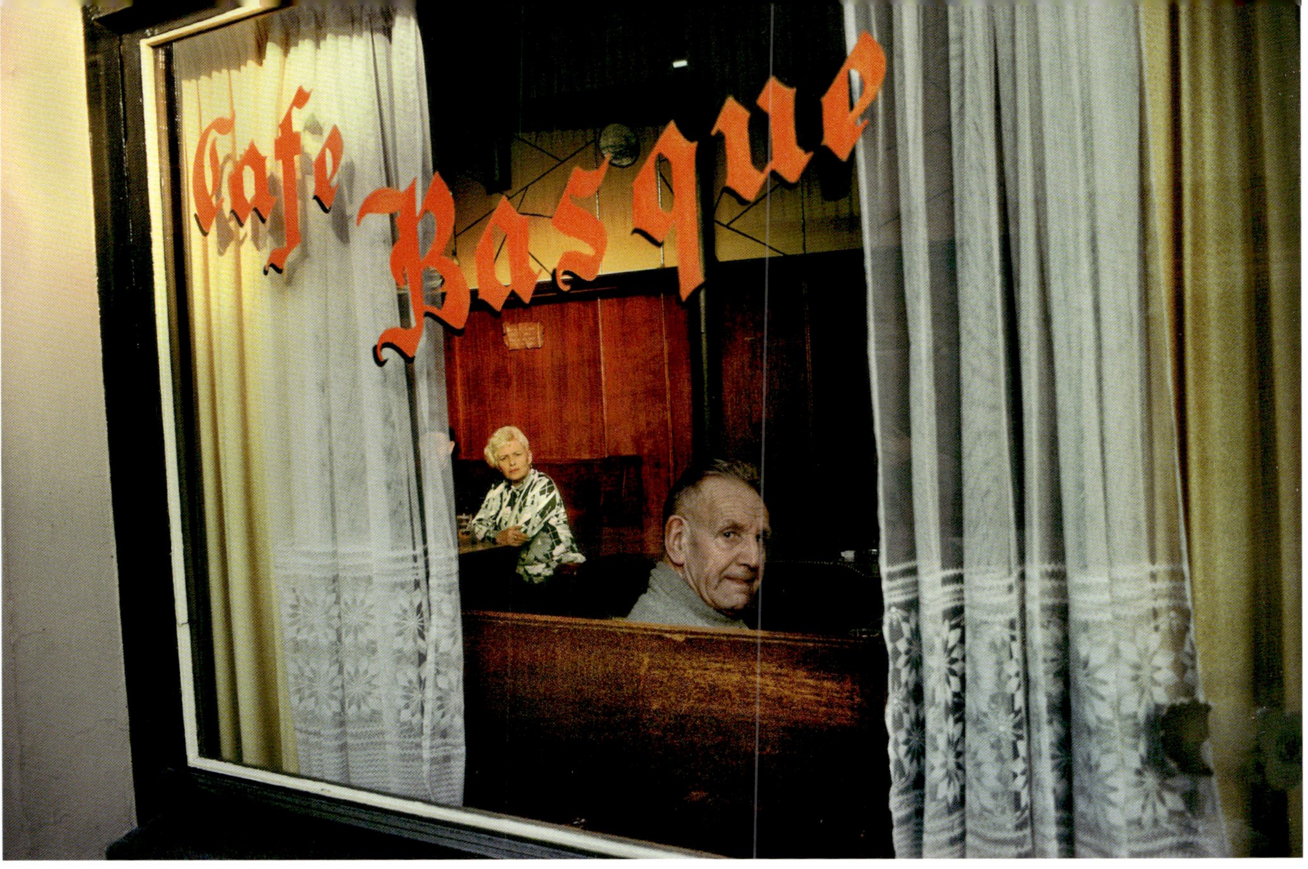
Cafe Basque

8. Antwerp, Belgium, 1992.

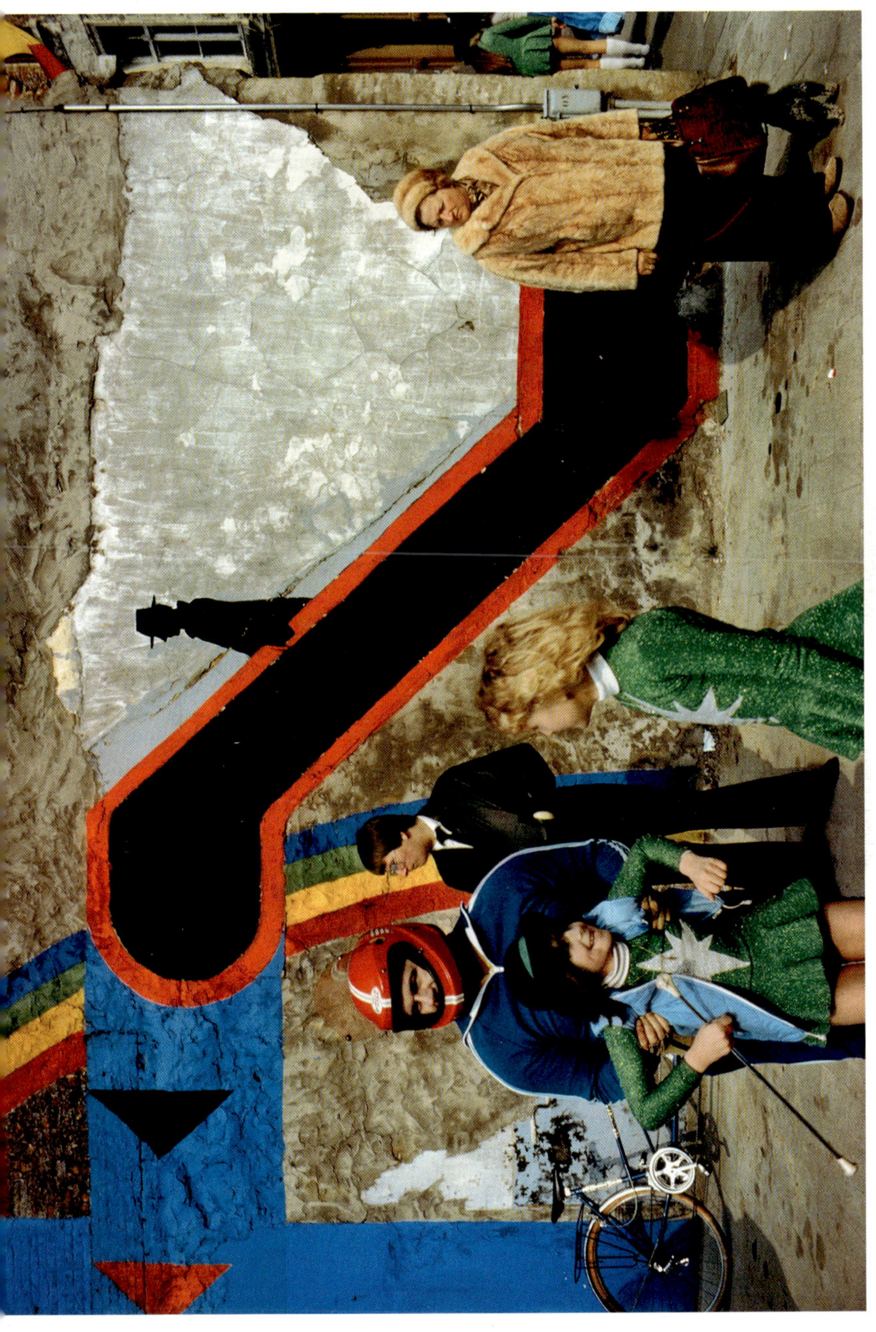

9. Belgium, 1988.

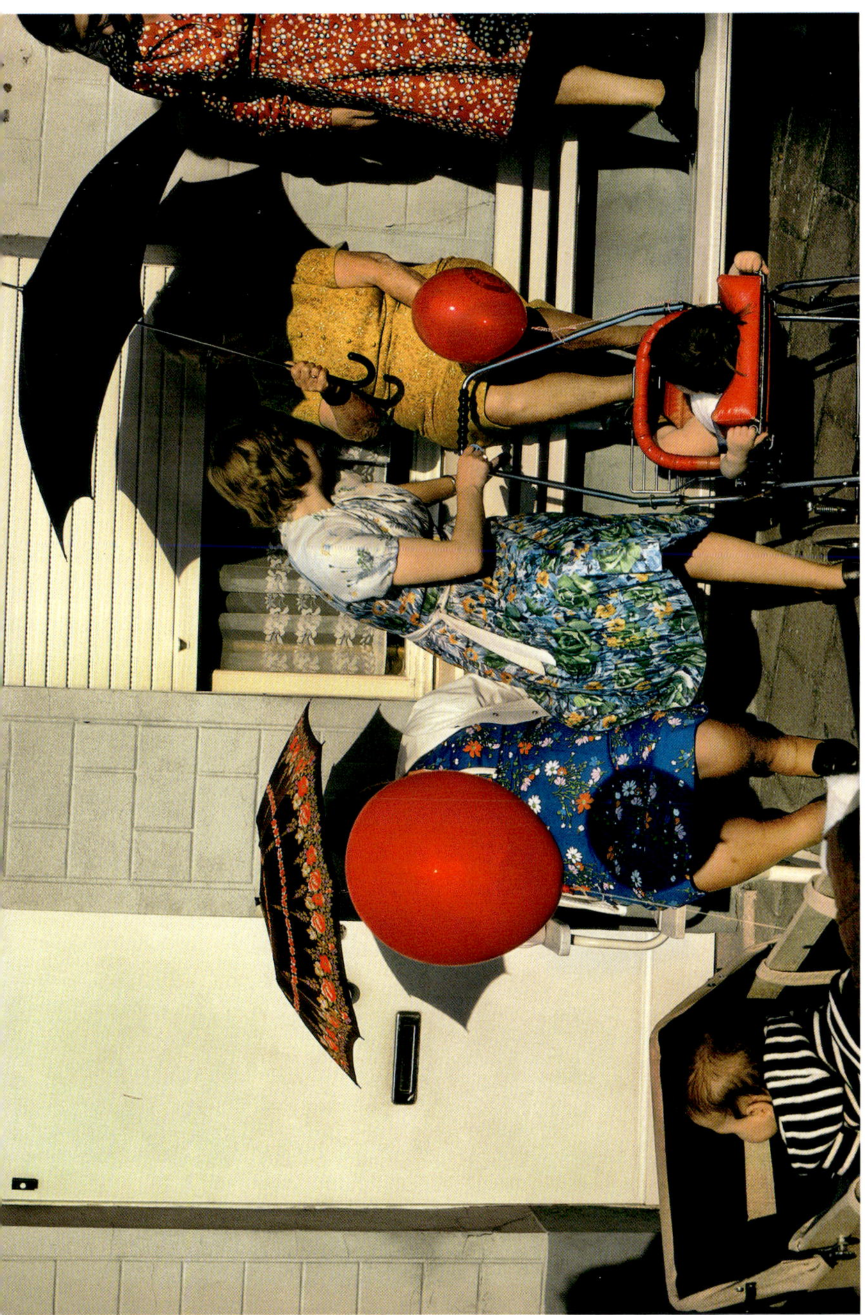

10. Manhattan, New York, 1982.

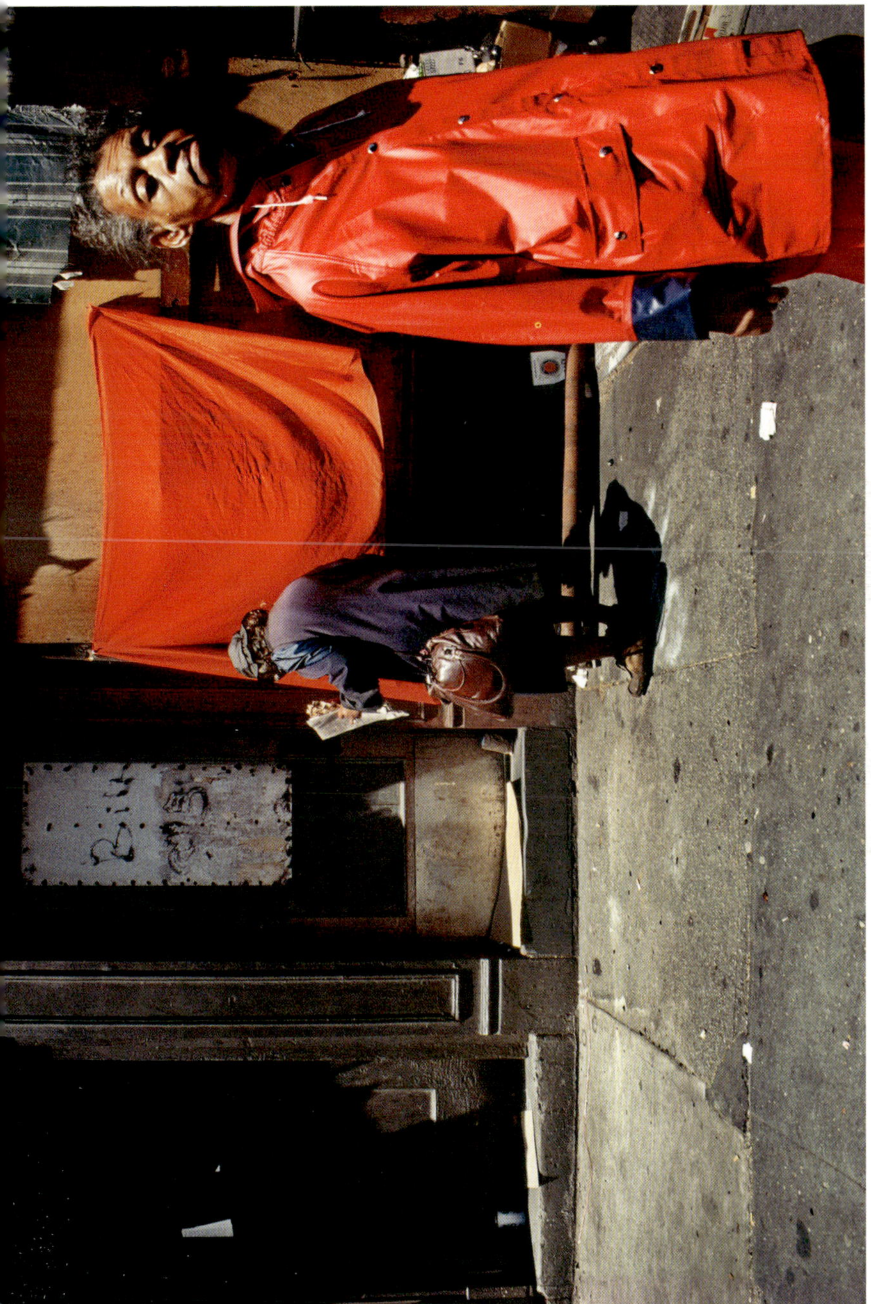

11. Brussels, 1981.

Overleaf:
12. Antwerp, Belgium, 1988.
13. La Courneuve, France, 1985.

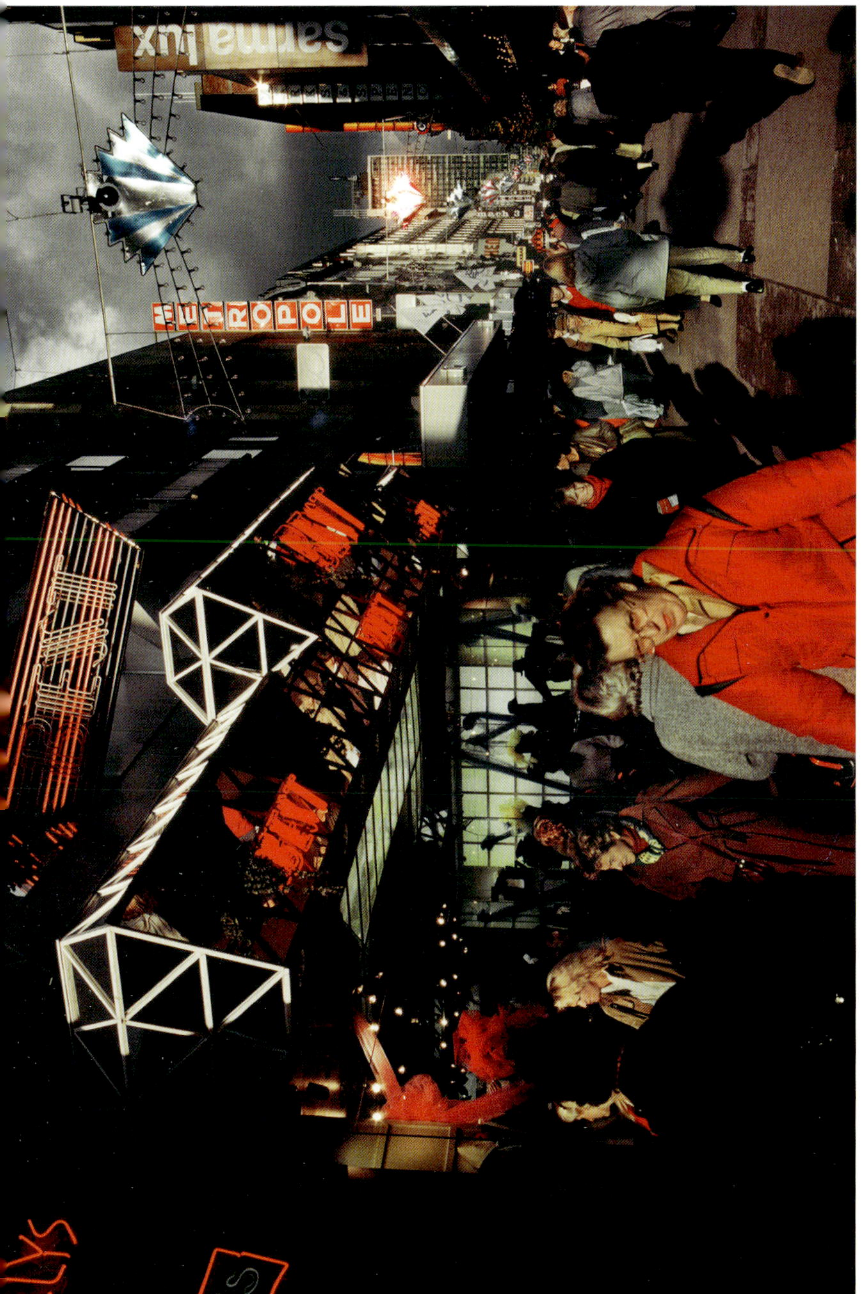

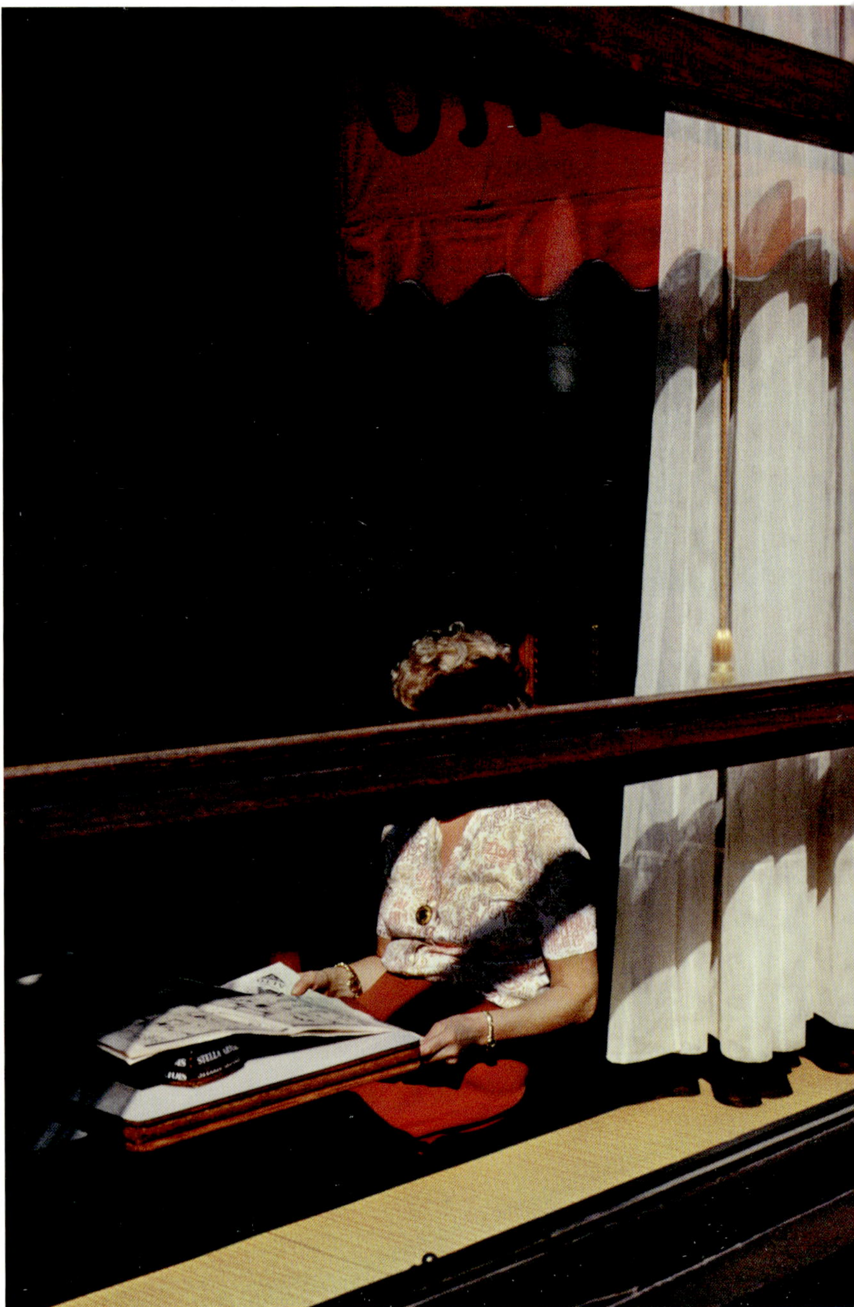

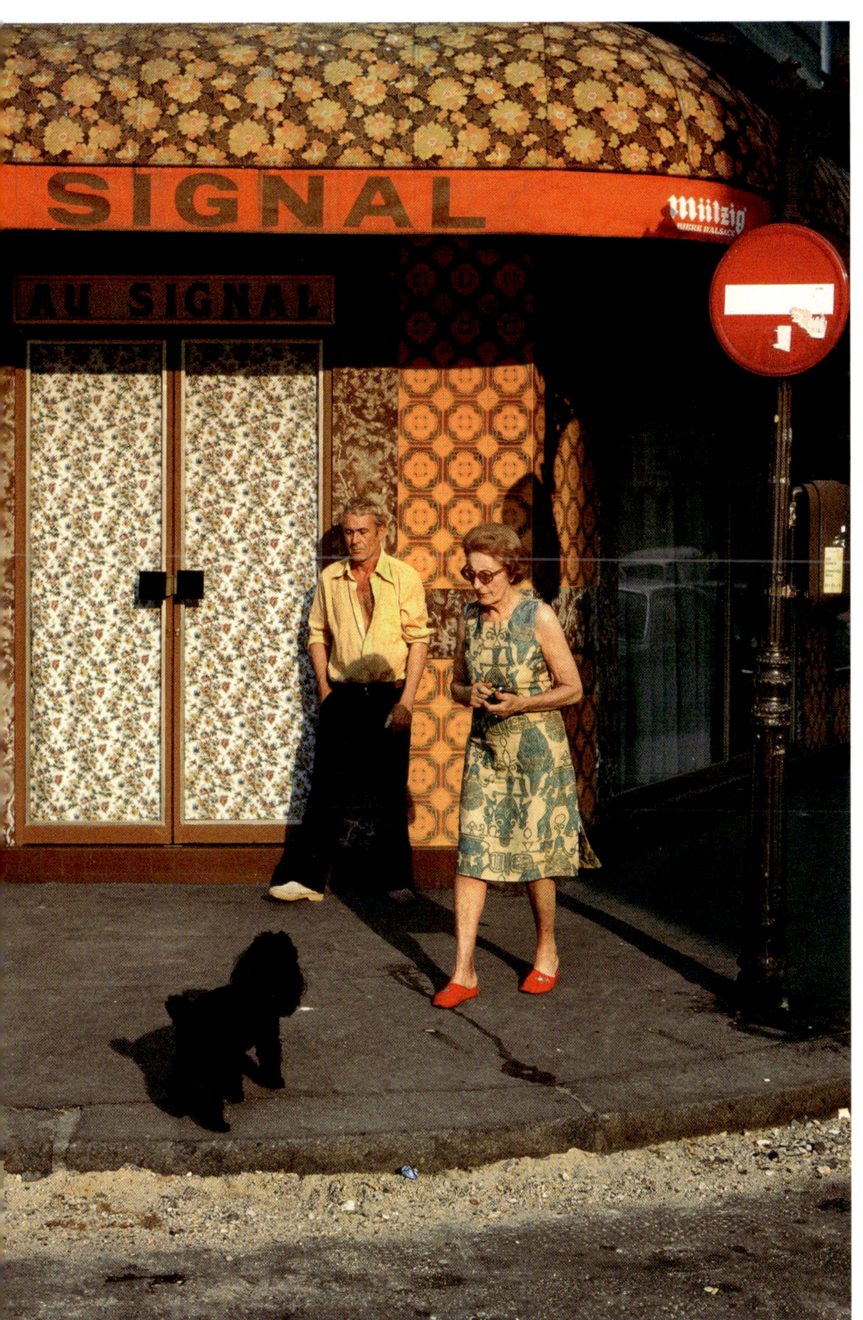

SIGNAL
Mützig
BIERE D'ALSACE
AU SIGNAL

14. Trans-Europe Express, Brussels–Paris, 1981.

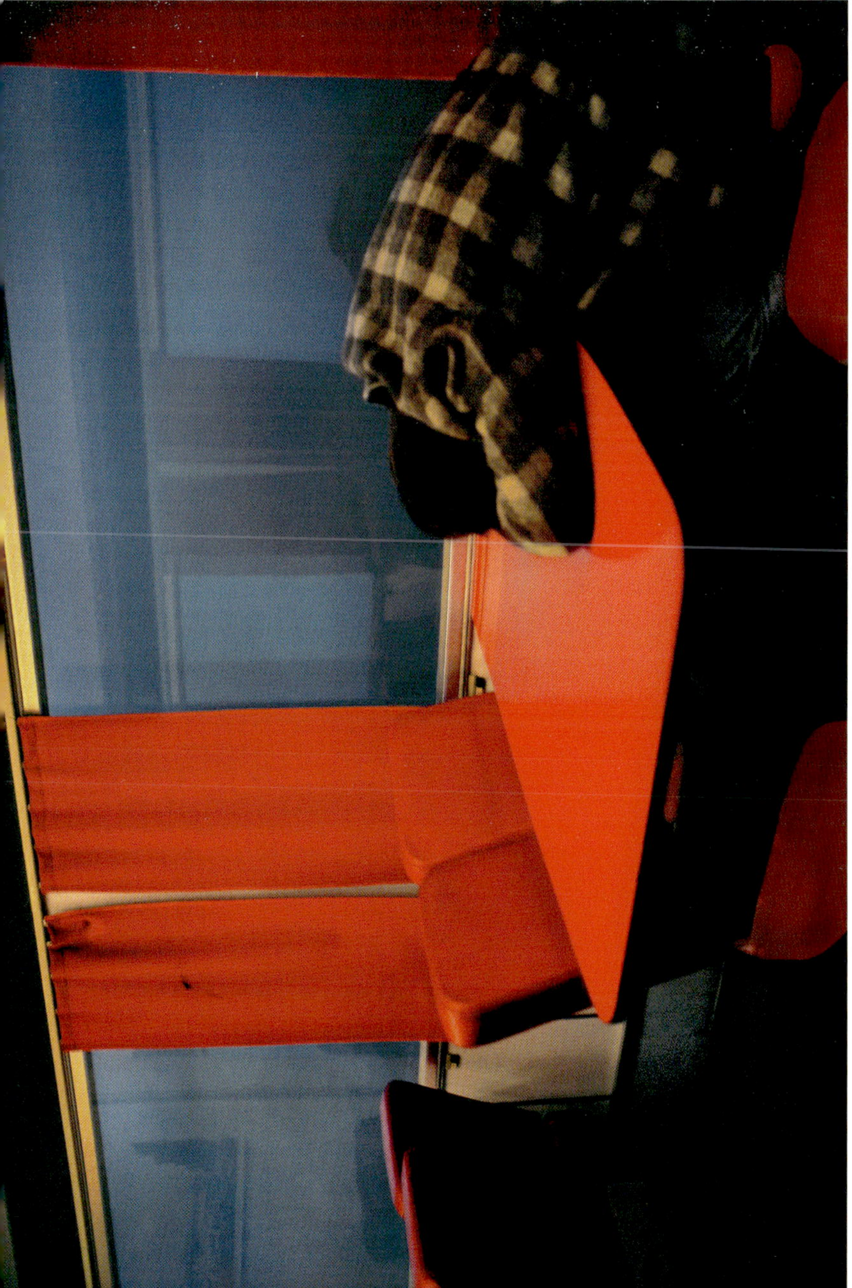

15. Los Angeles, 1982.

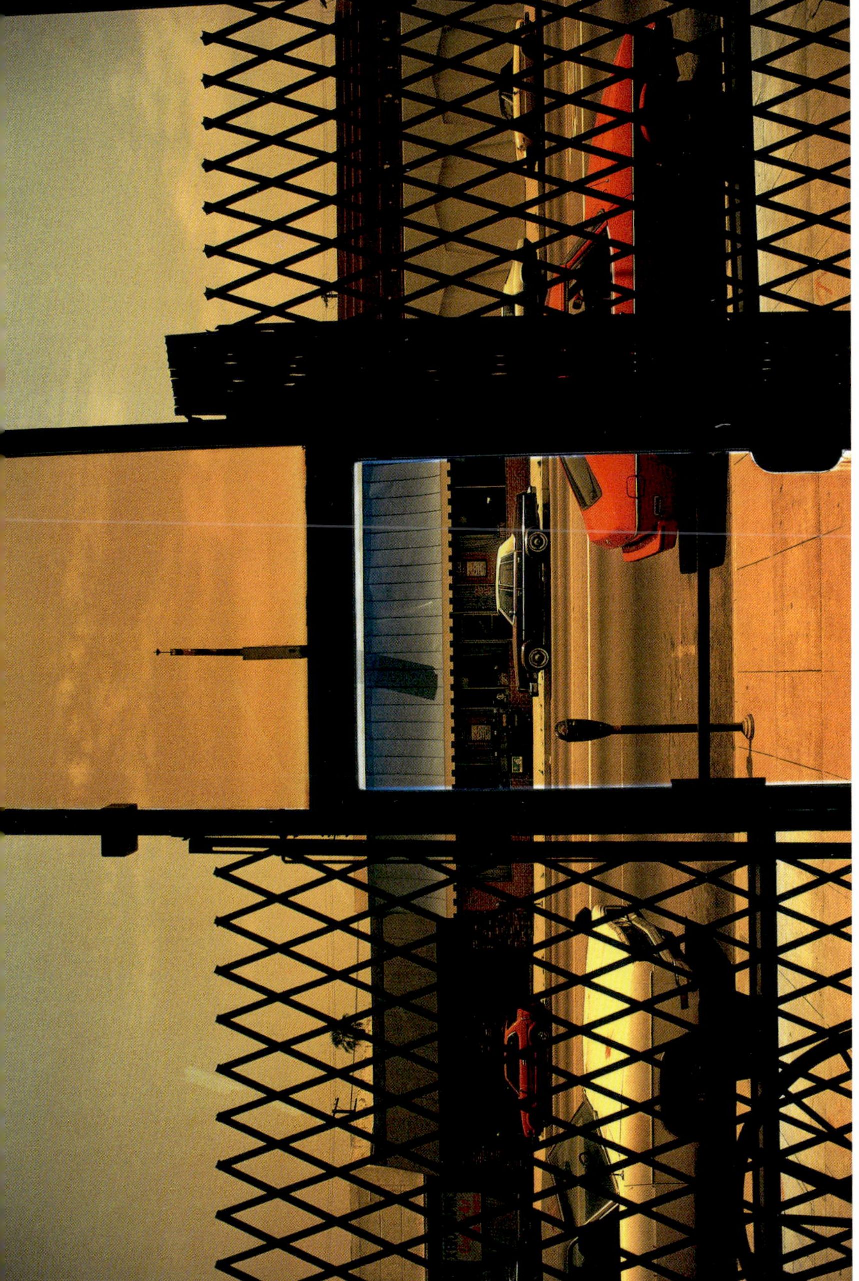

16. Belgium, 2014.

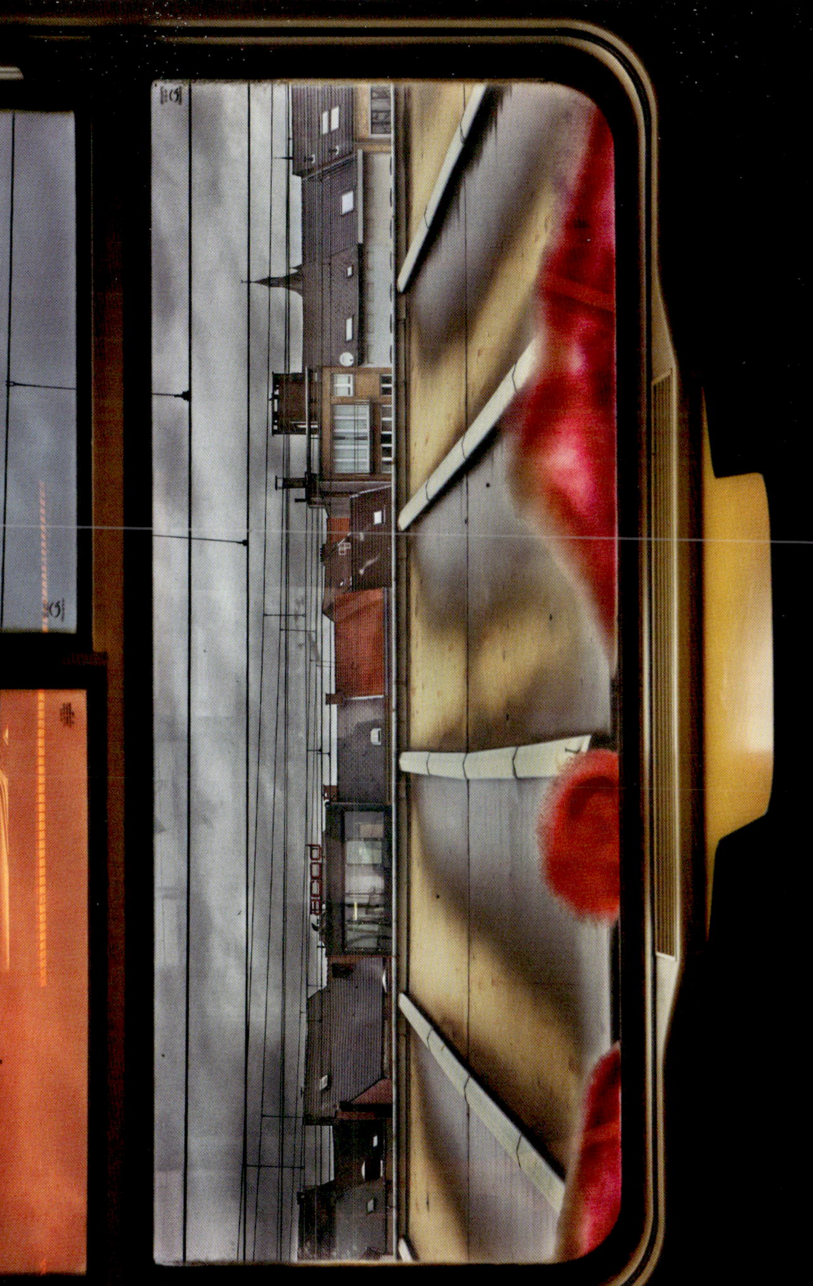

17. Ostend, Belgium, 1988.

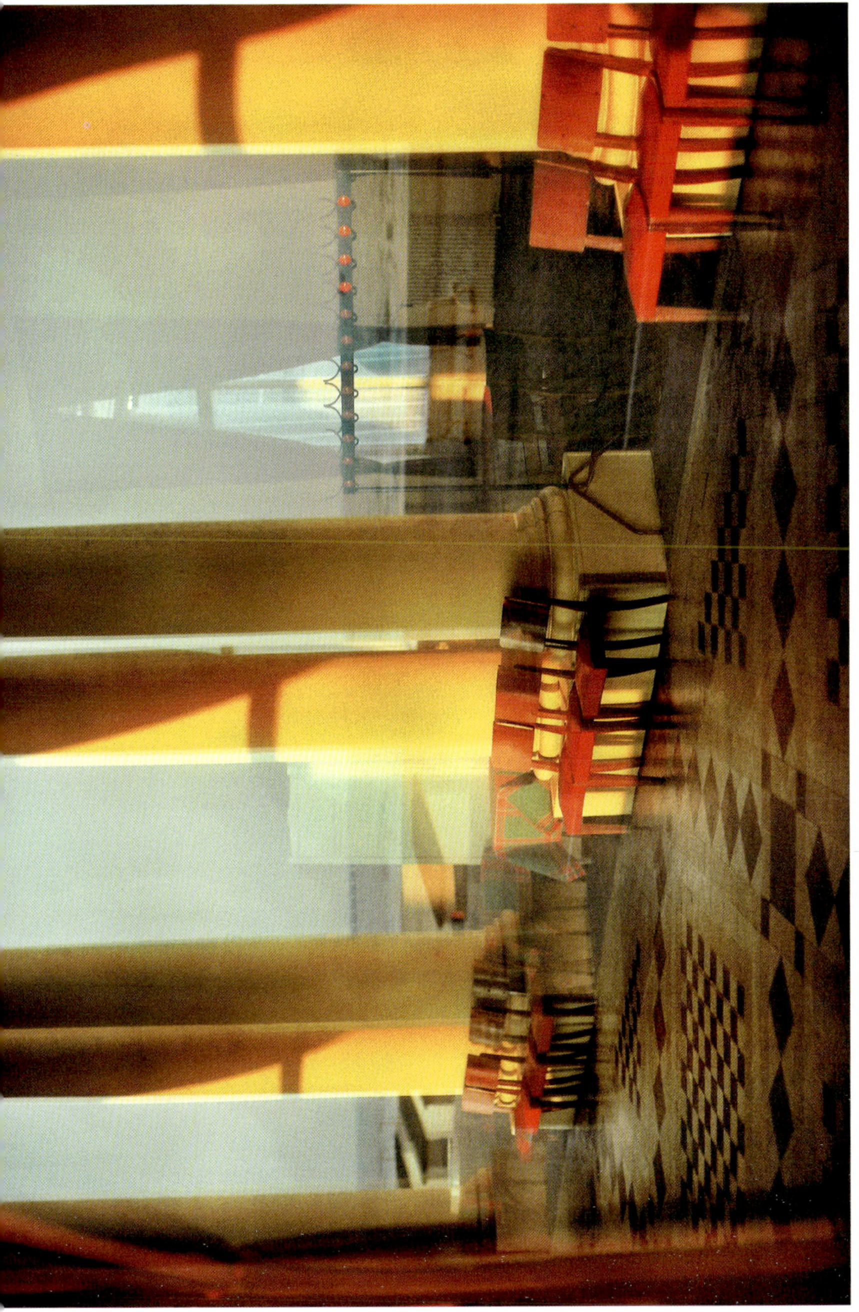

18. Ostend, Belgium, 1988.

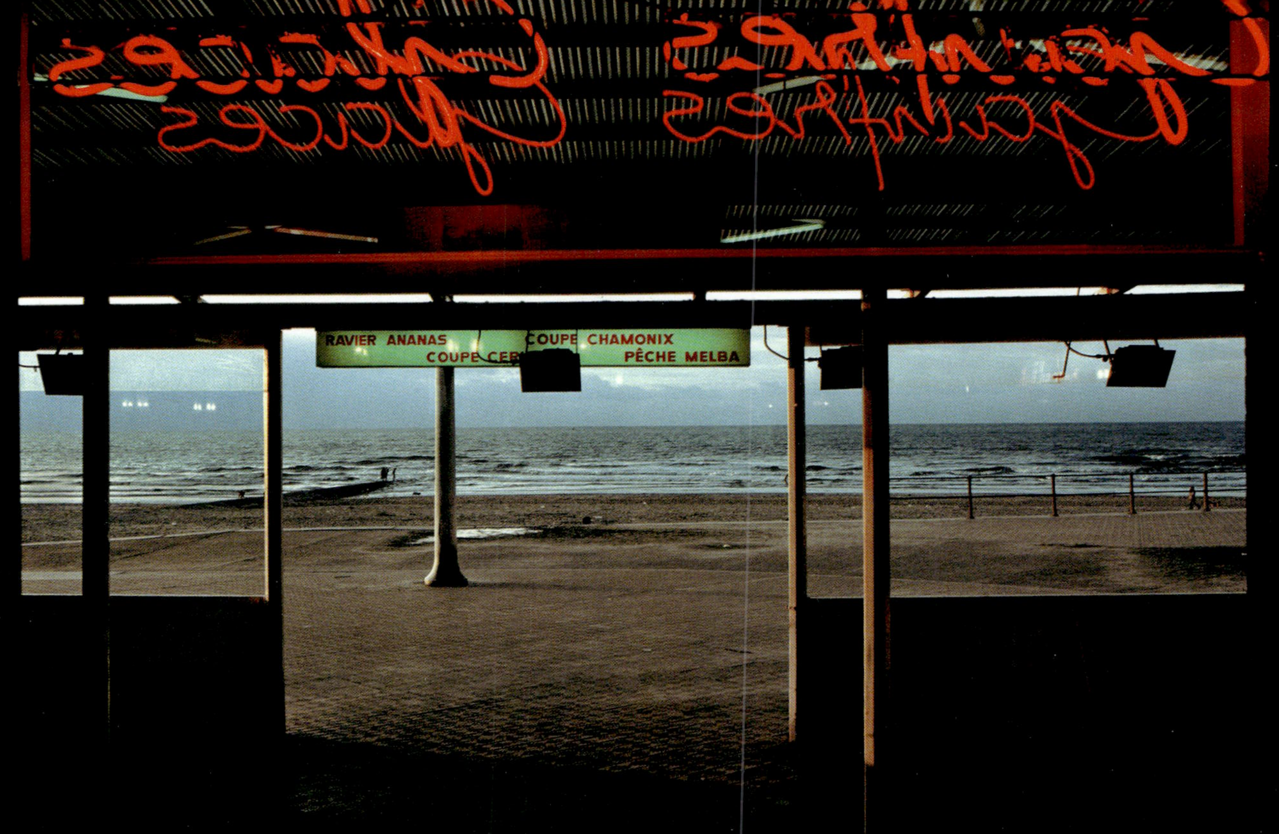

RAVIER ANANAS   COUPE CHAMONIX
COUPE CER   PÊCHE MELBA

19. Las Vegas, 1982.

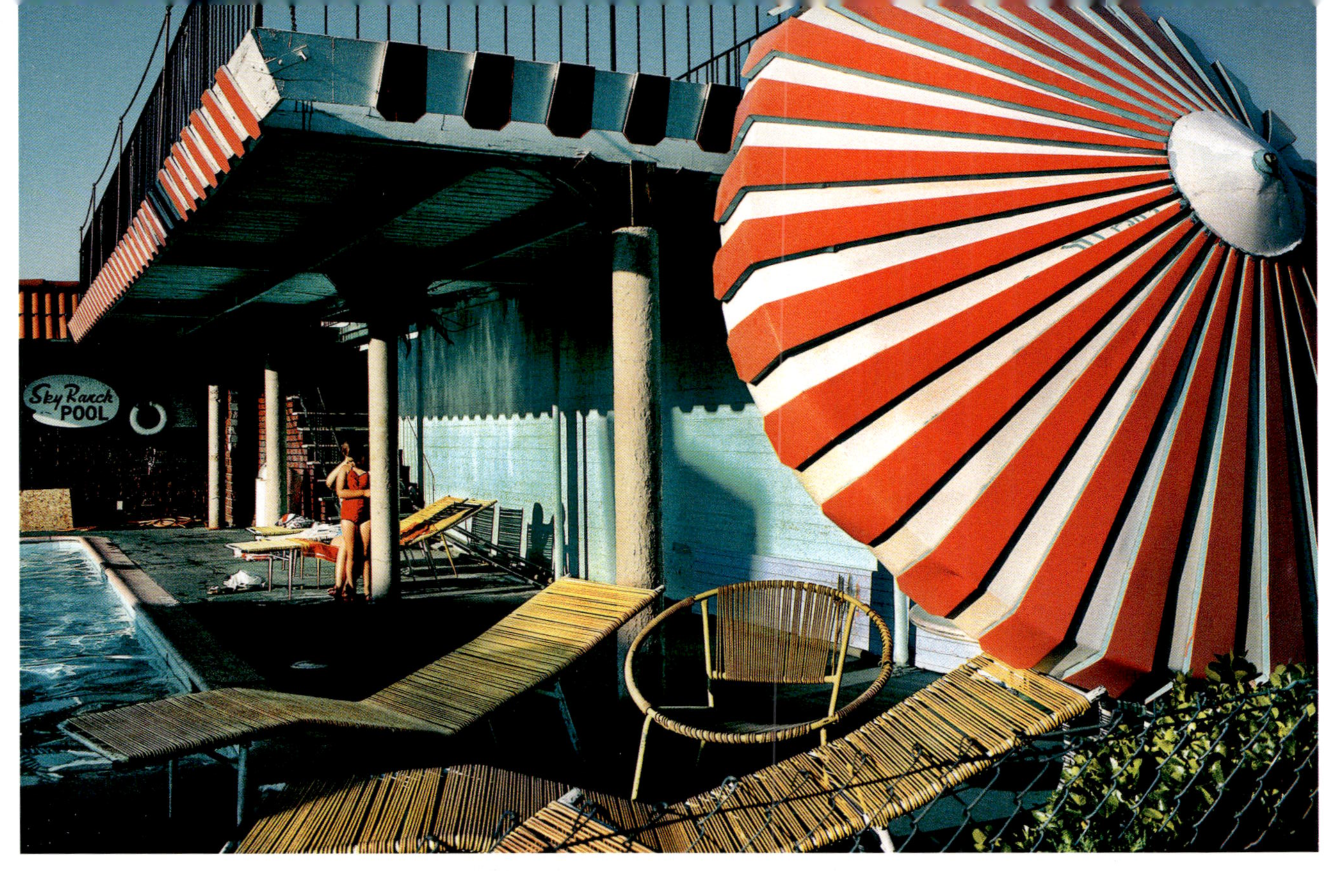

Sky Ranch
POOL

20. Suburbs of Las Vegas, 1982.

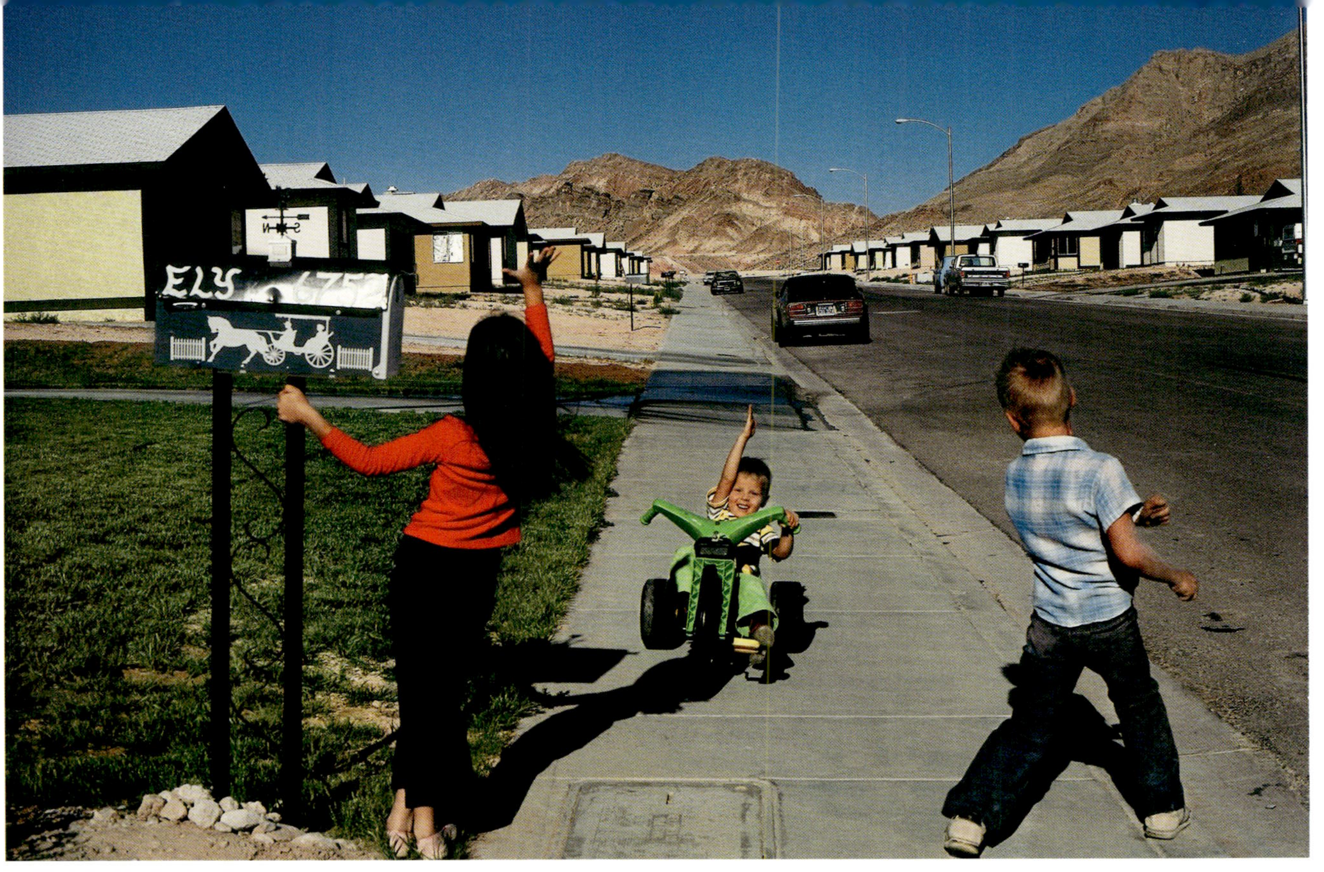
ELY
6752

21. Nevada, 1982.

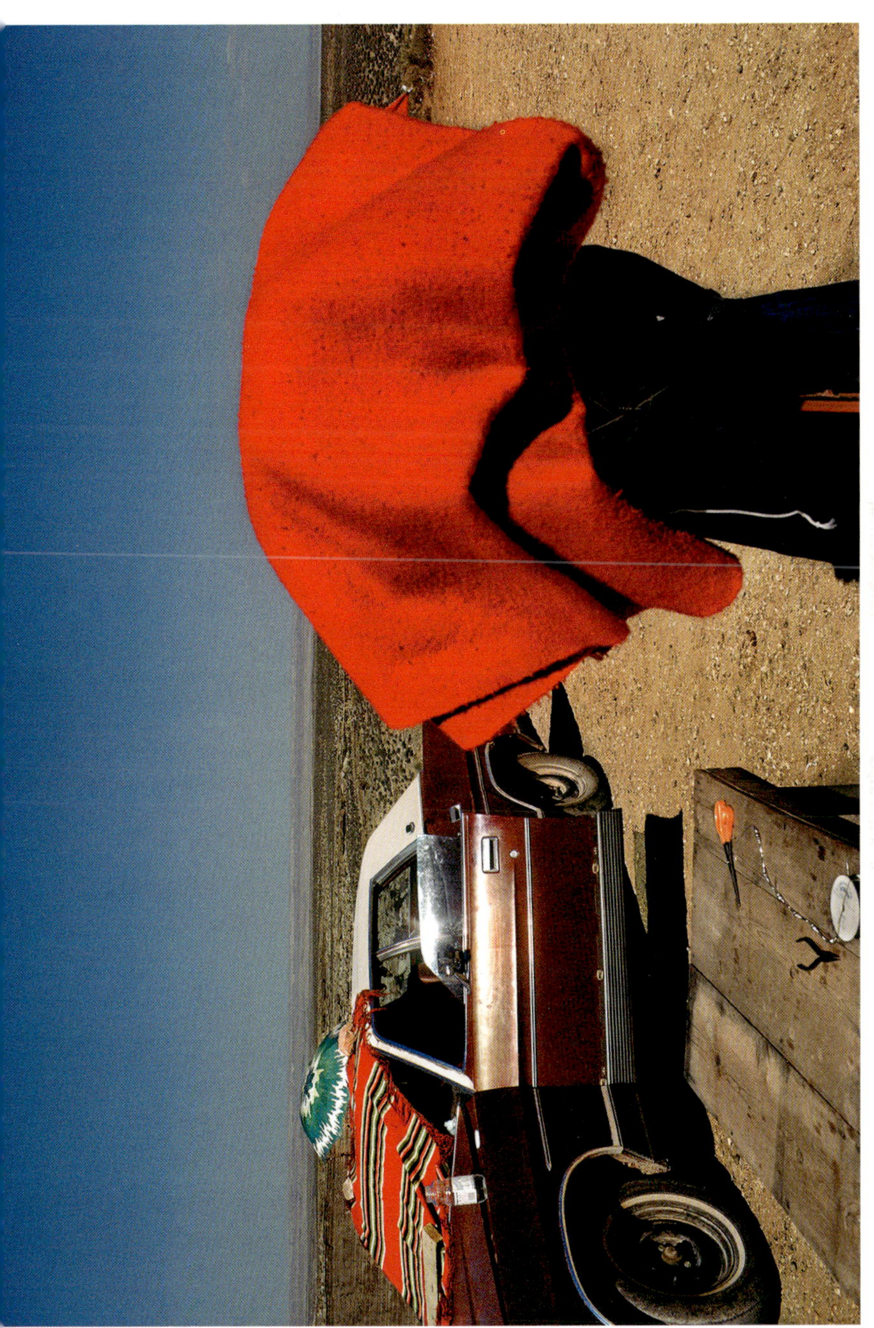

22. Flower market by the Seine, Paris, 1985.

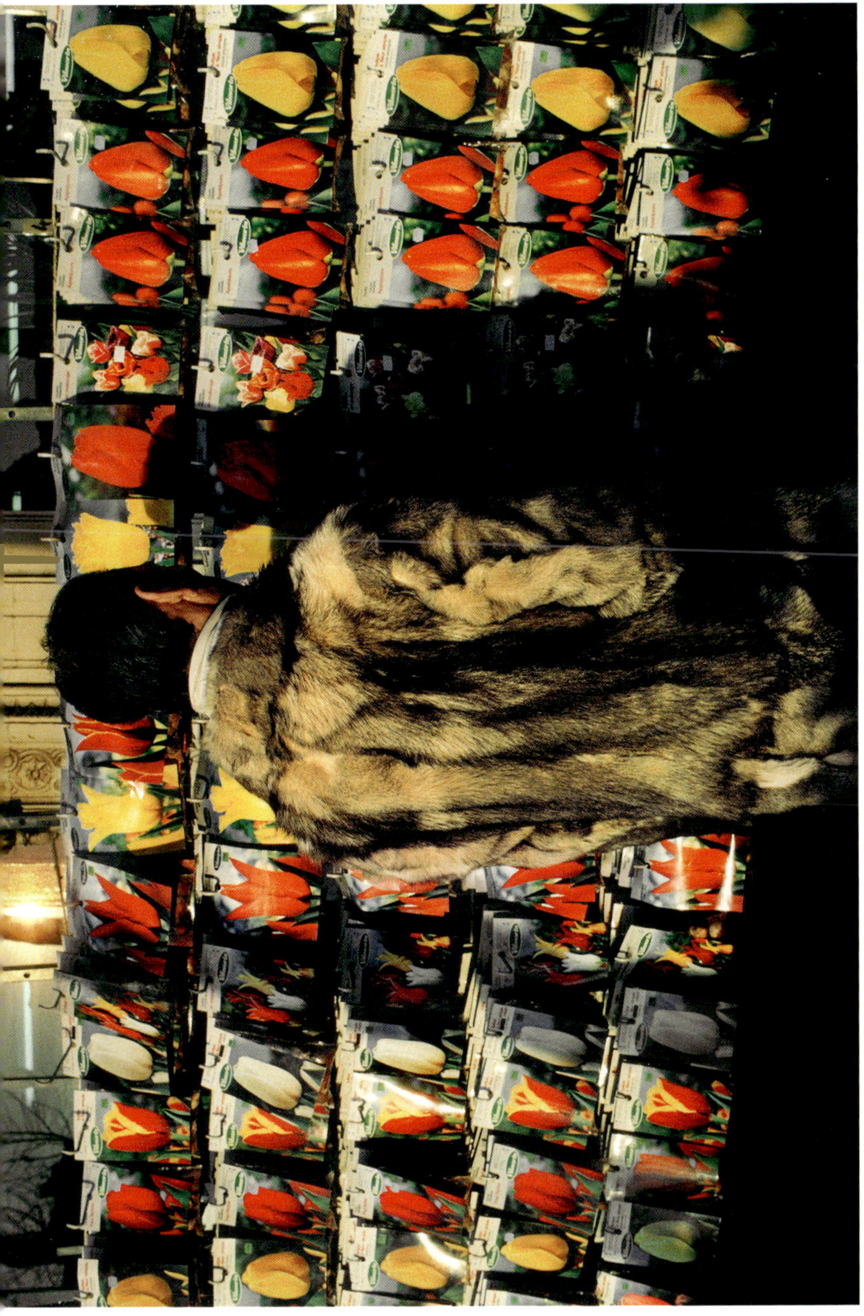

23. Palais des Beaux-Arts, Brussels, 1981.

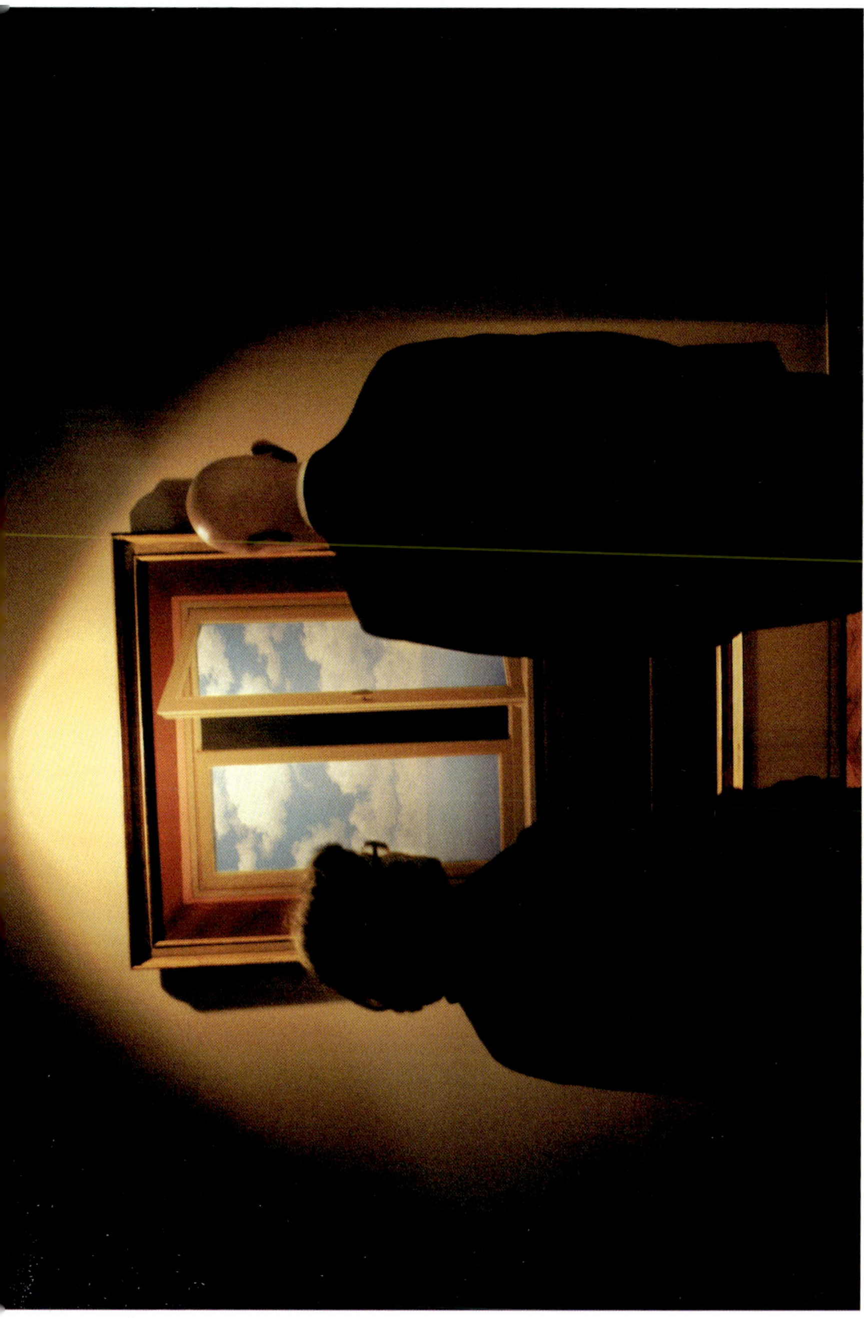

24. Malmö, Sweden, 1982.

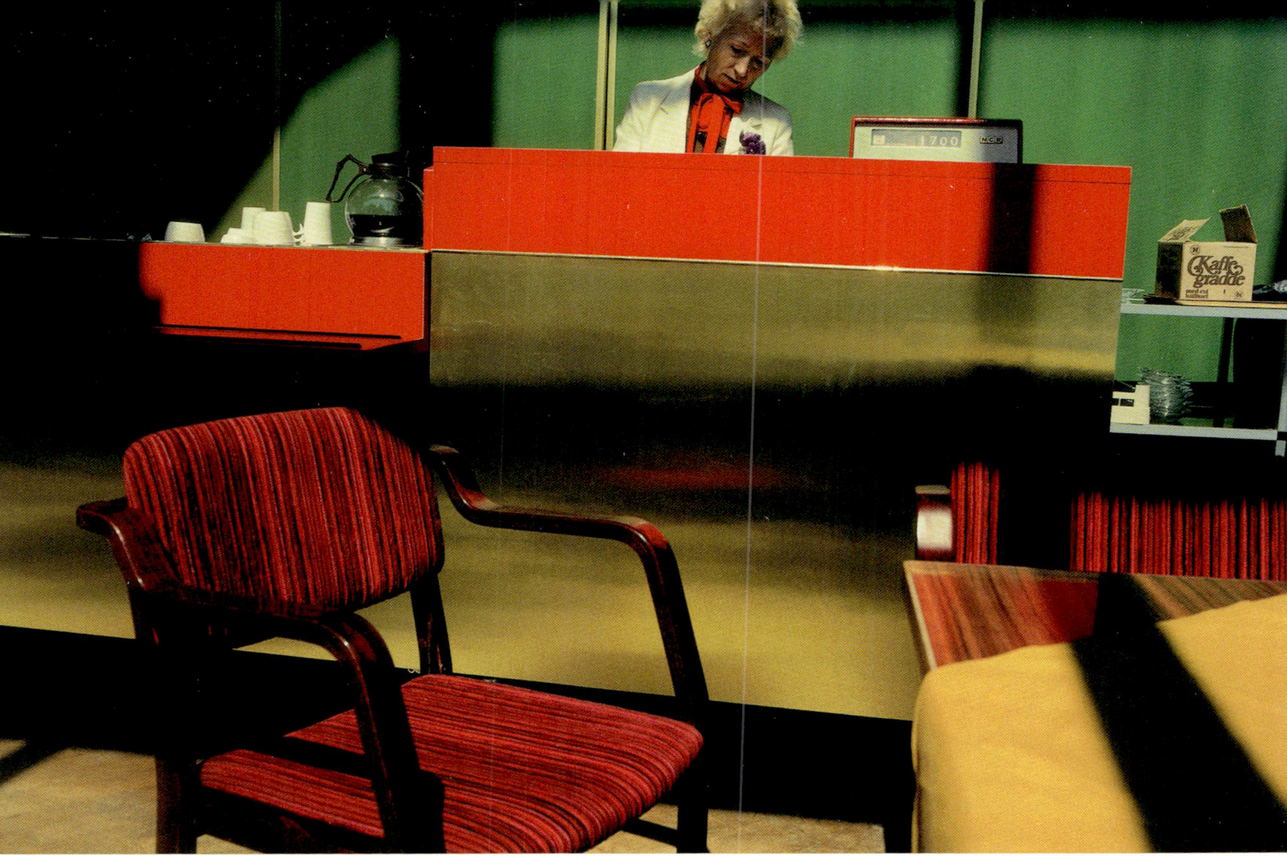

1700   NCR
Kaffe
grädde

25. Paris, 1985.

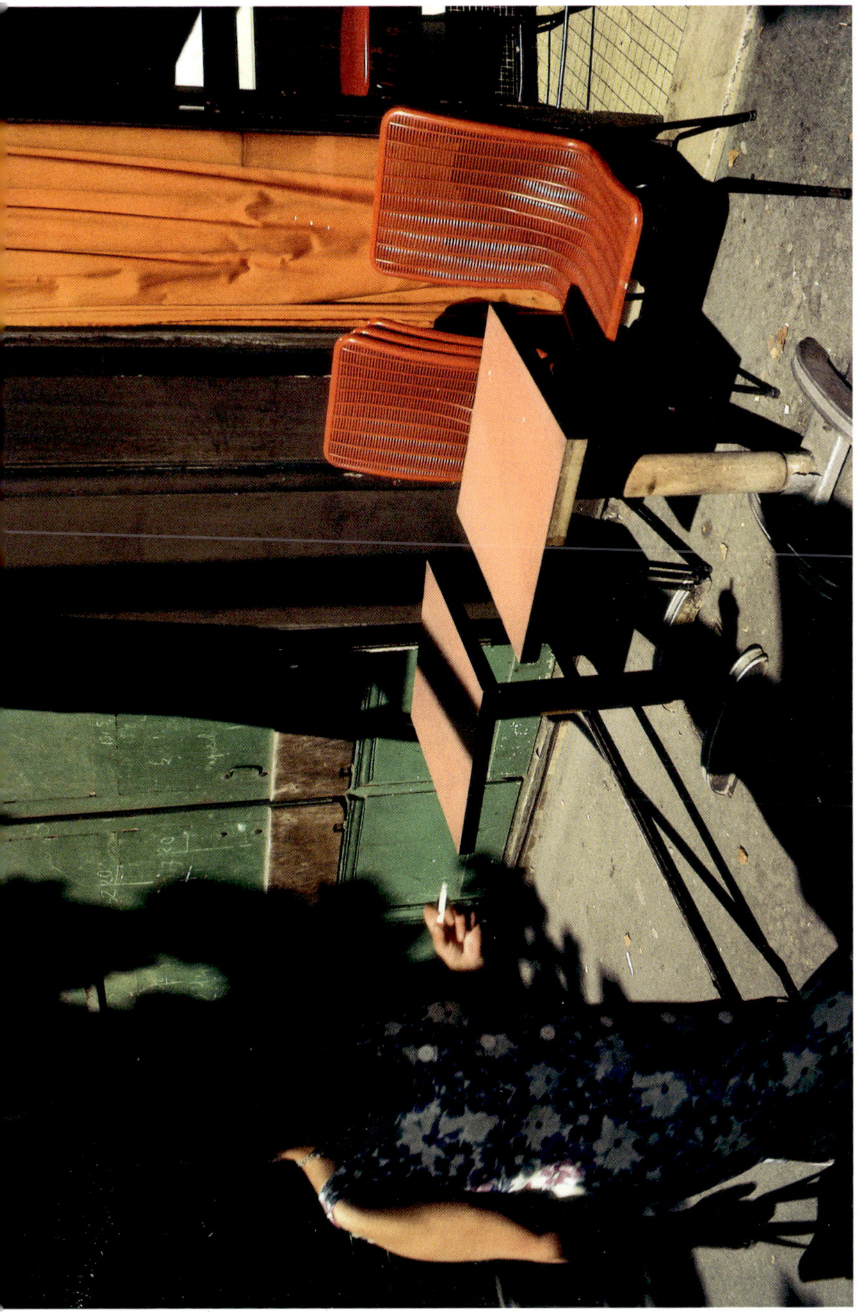

26. Souk, Meknes, Morocco, 1988.

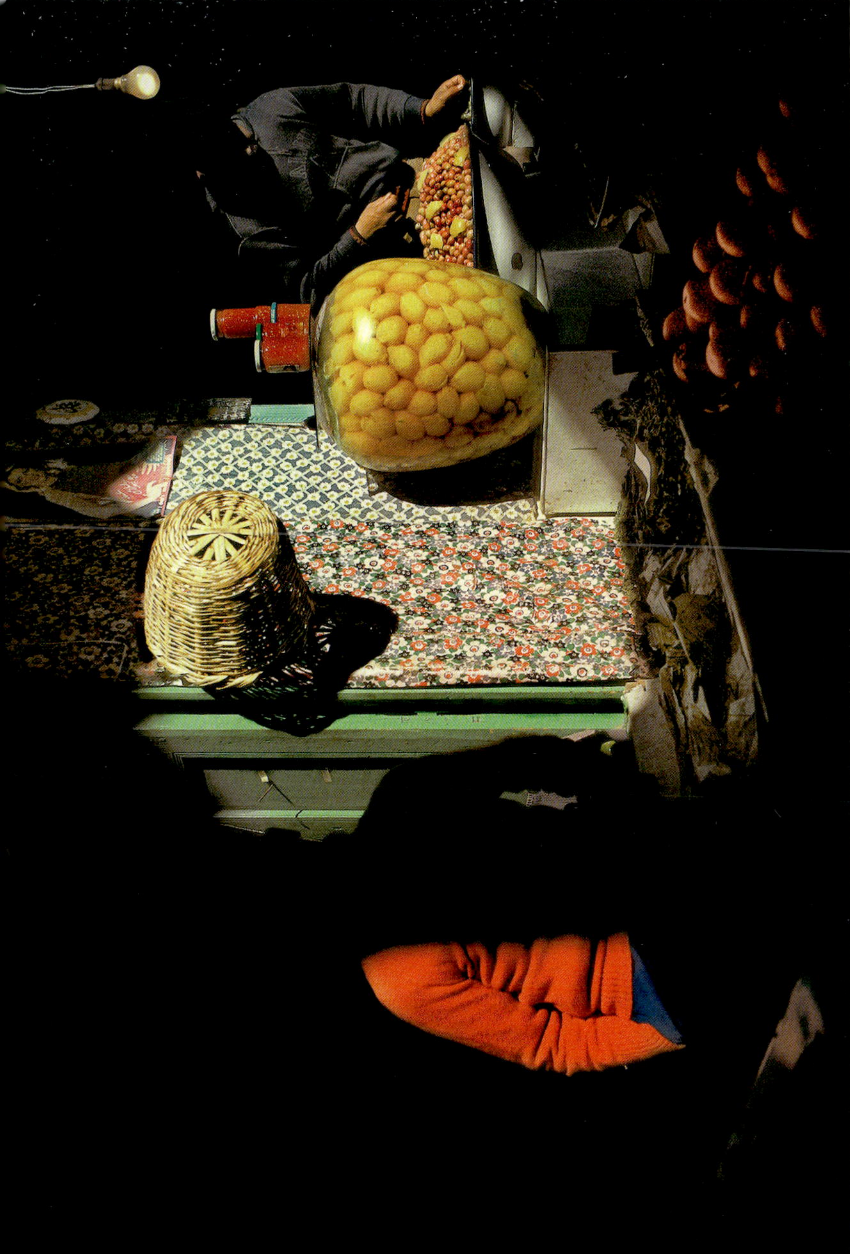

27. Montreal, 1998.

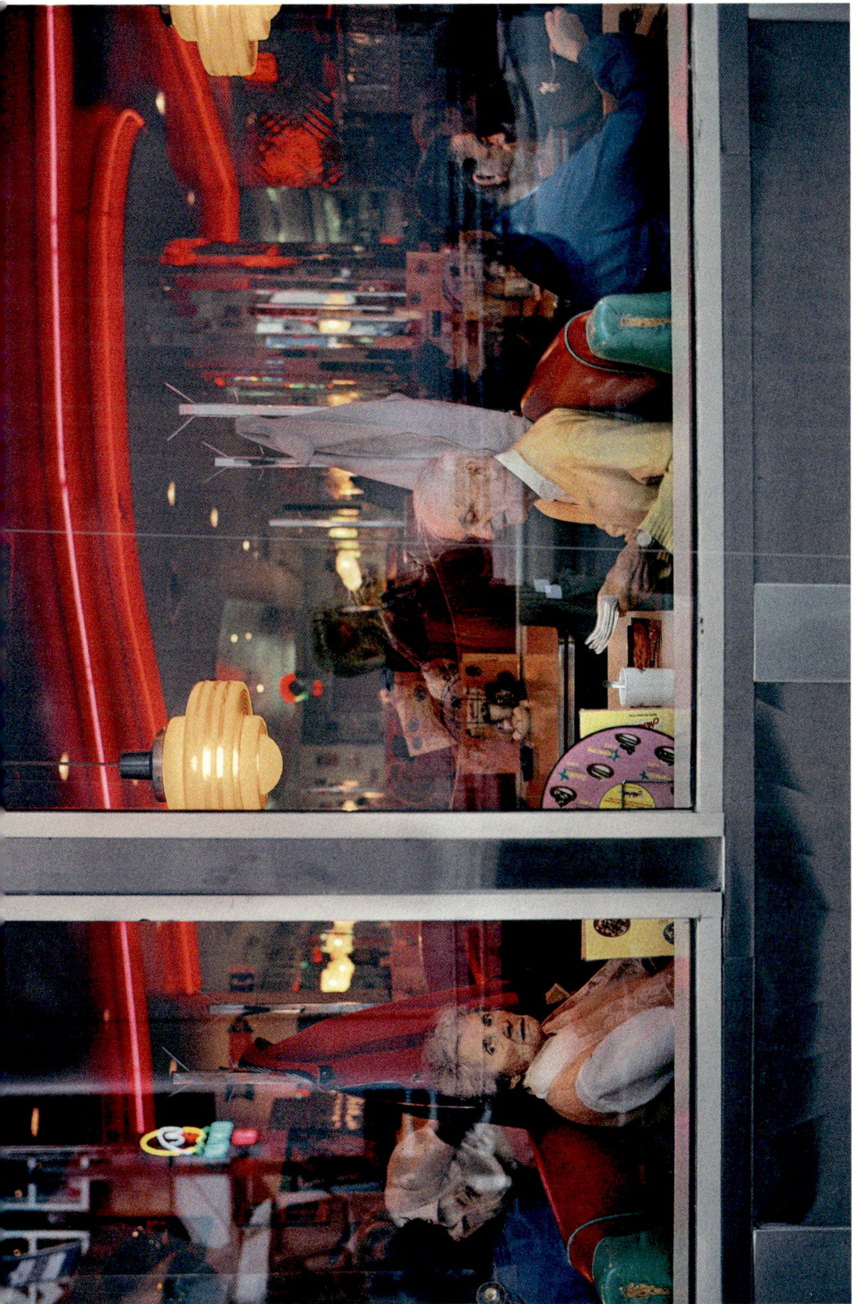

28. Paris, 2019.

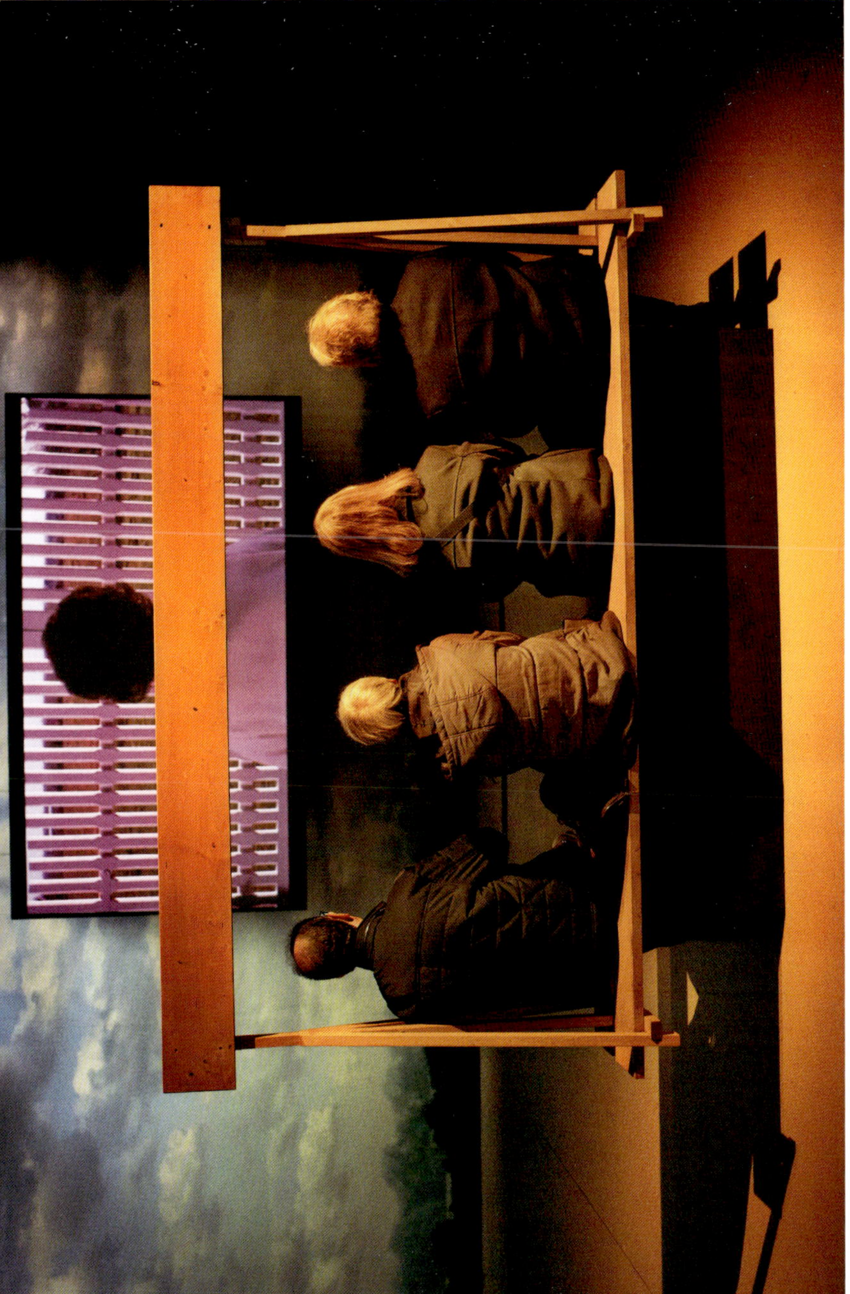

29. Antwerp, Belgium, 1992.

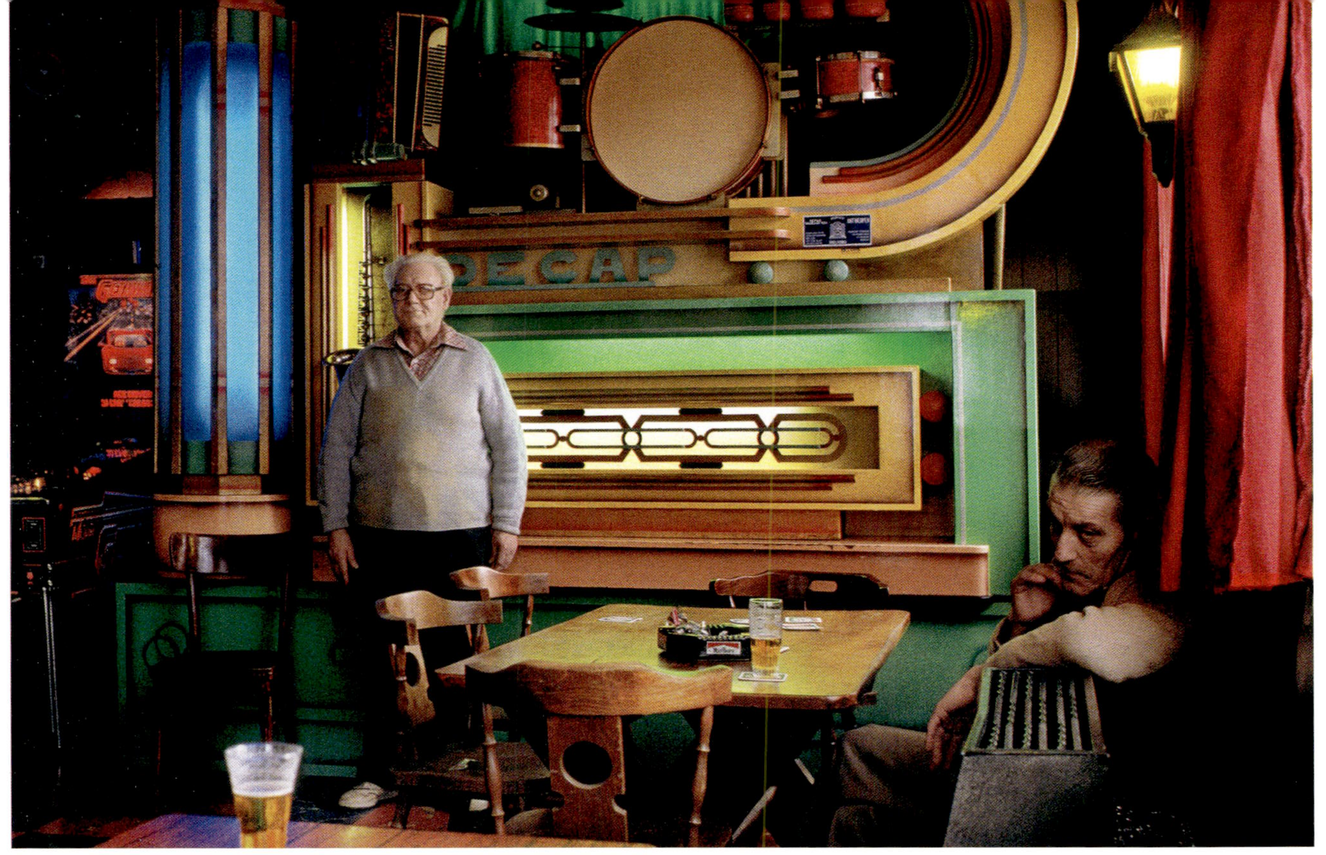
DECAP

30. Liège, Belgium, 1981.

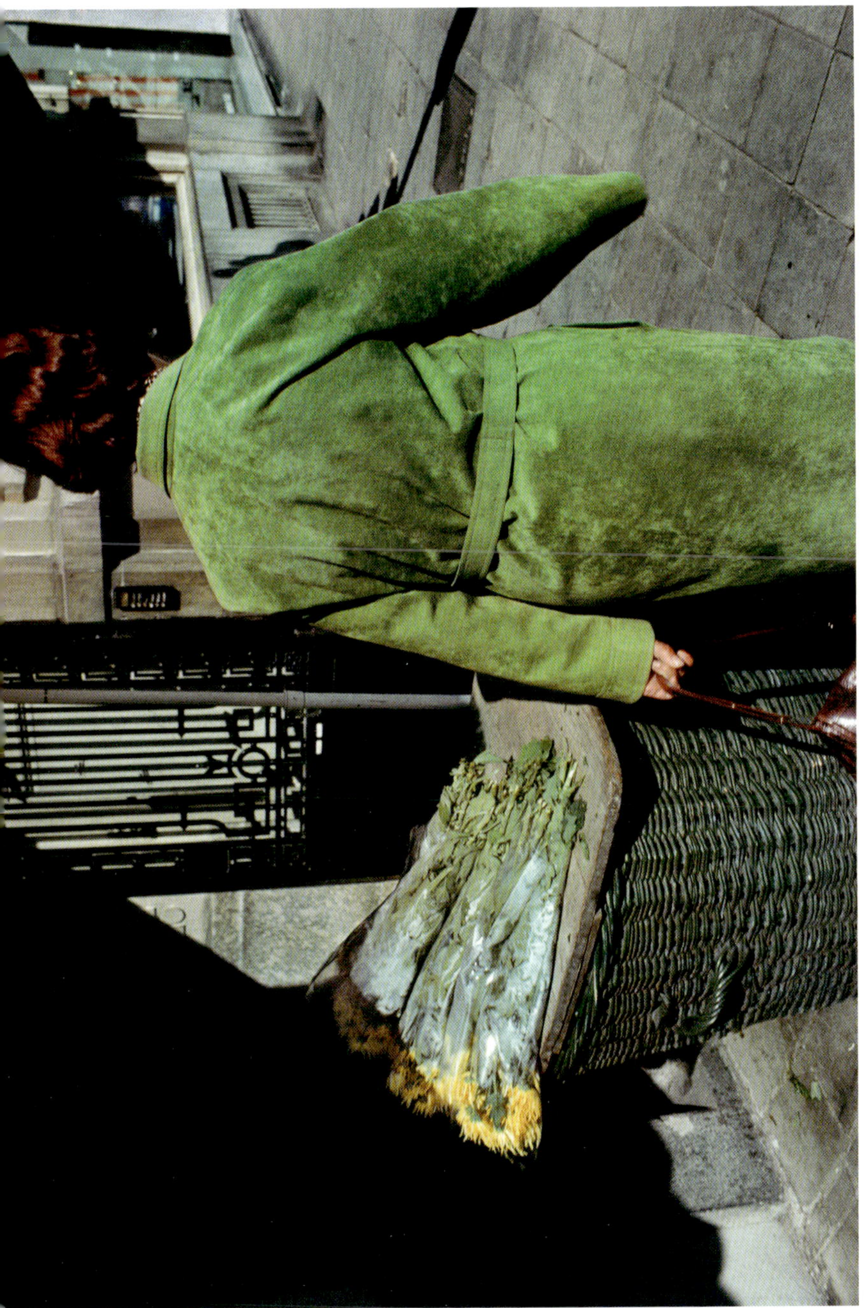

31. Brussels, 1981.

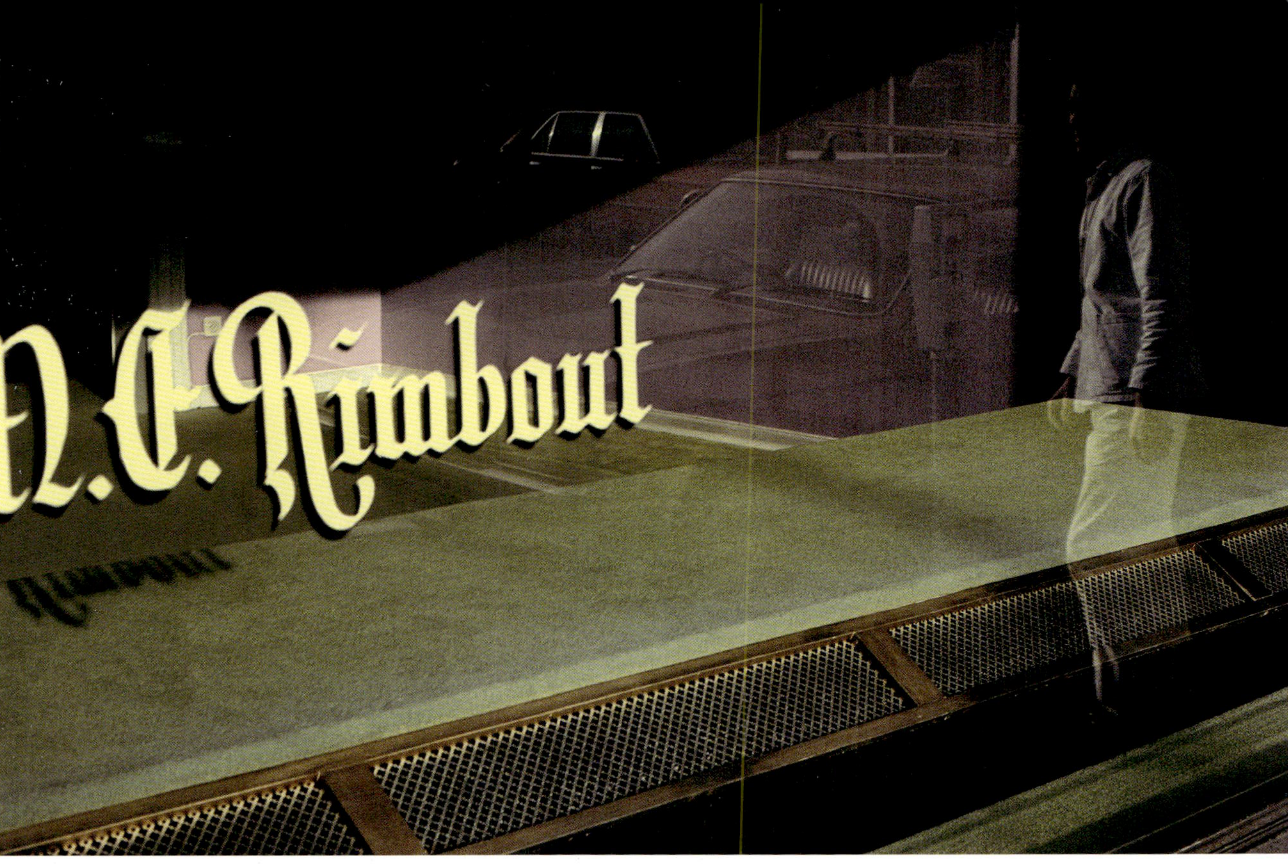
L.C. Rimbout

32. Washington DC, 1986.

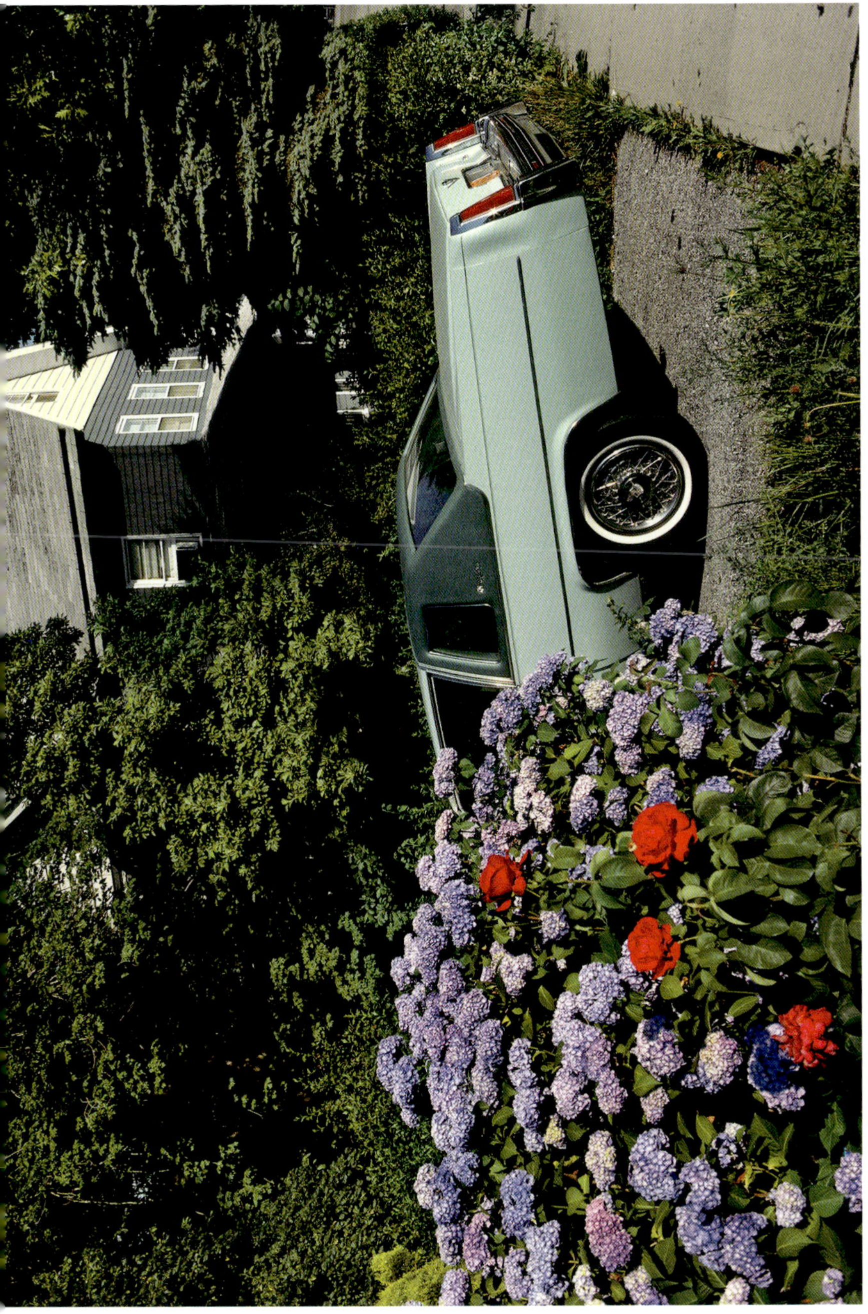

33. Moscow, 1989.

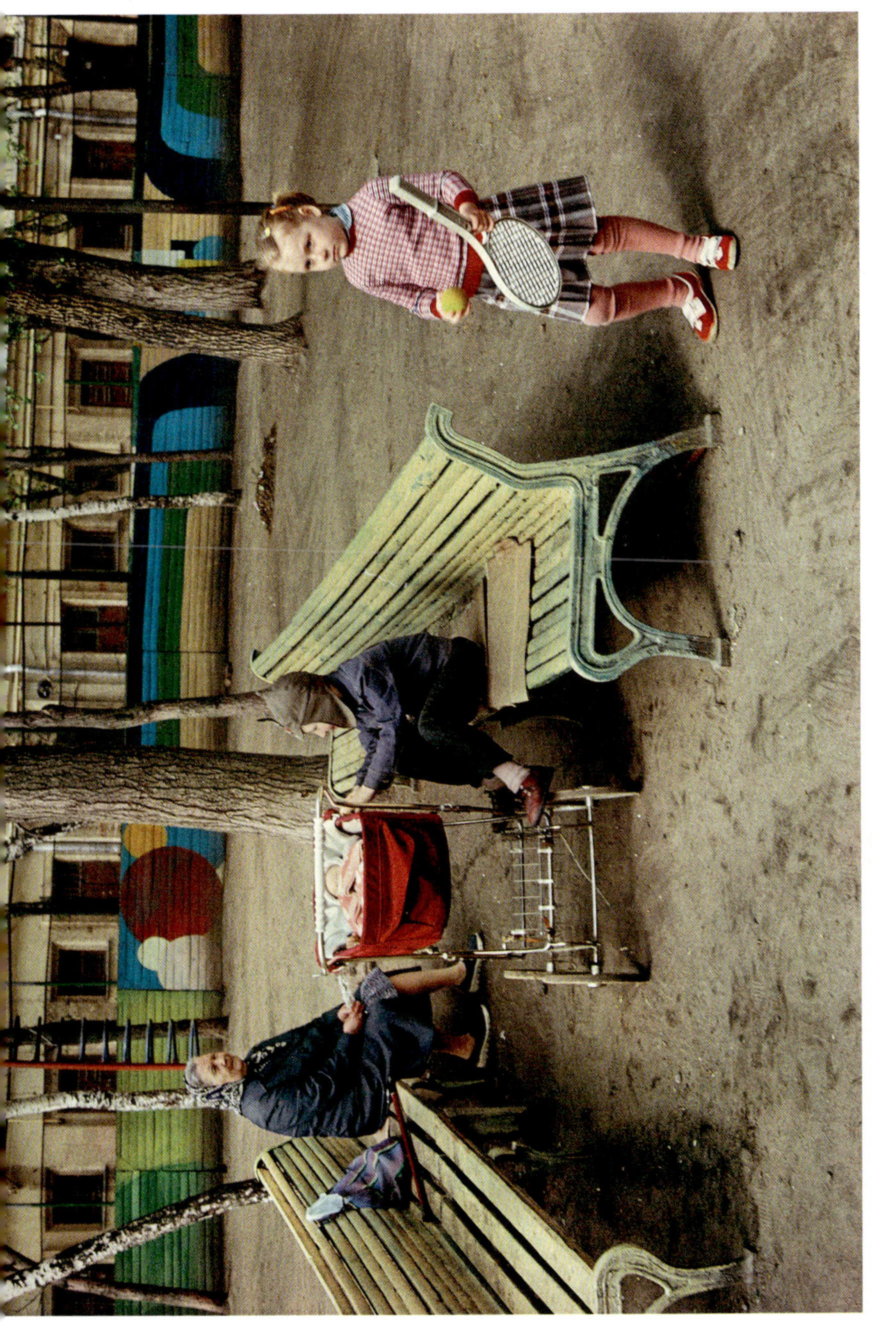

34. Estremadura, Spain, 1998.

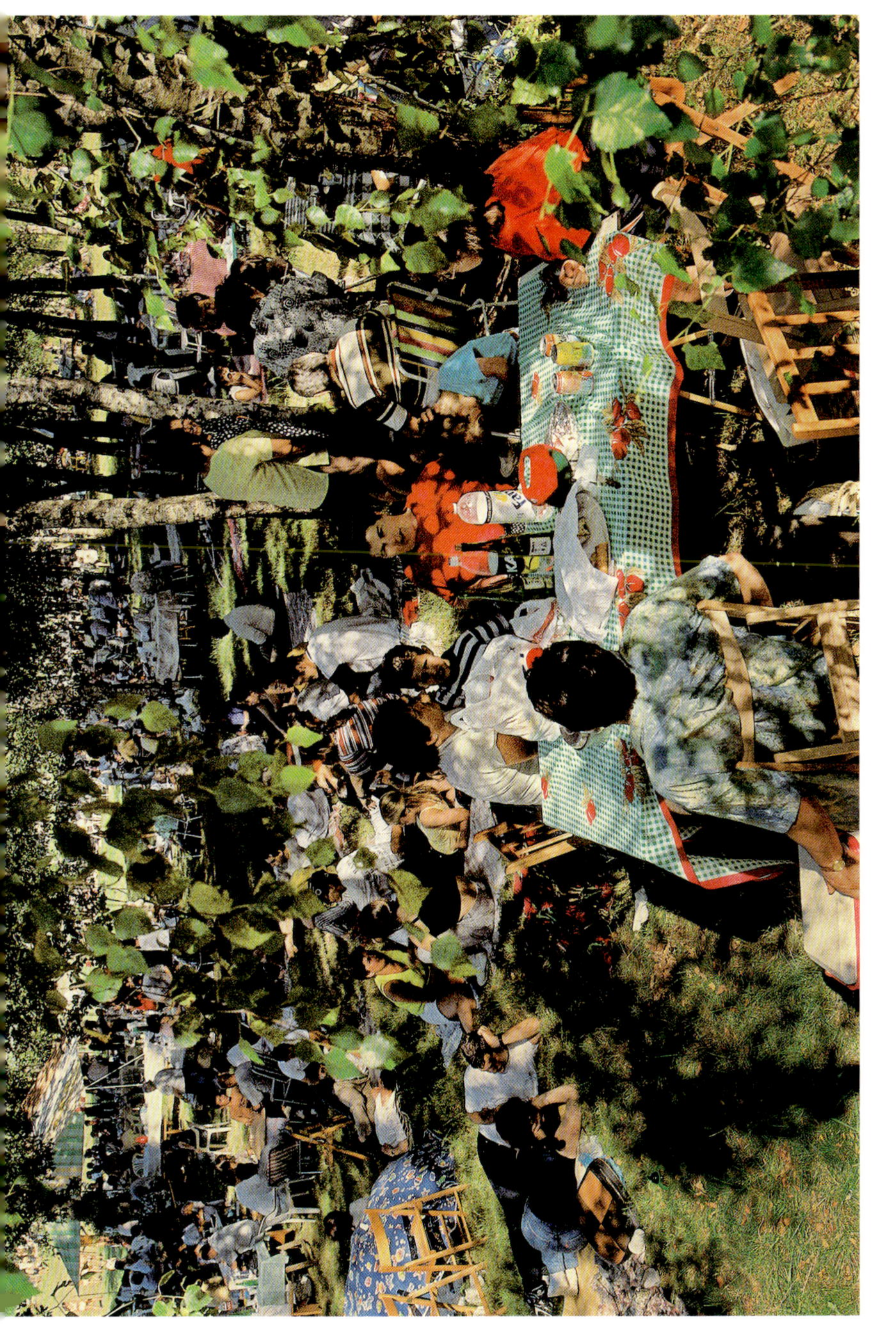

35. County Kerry, Ireland, 1984.

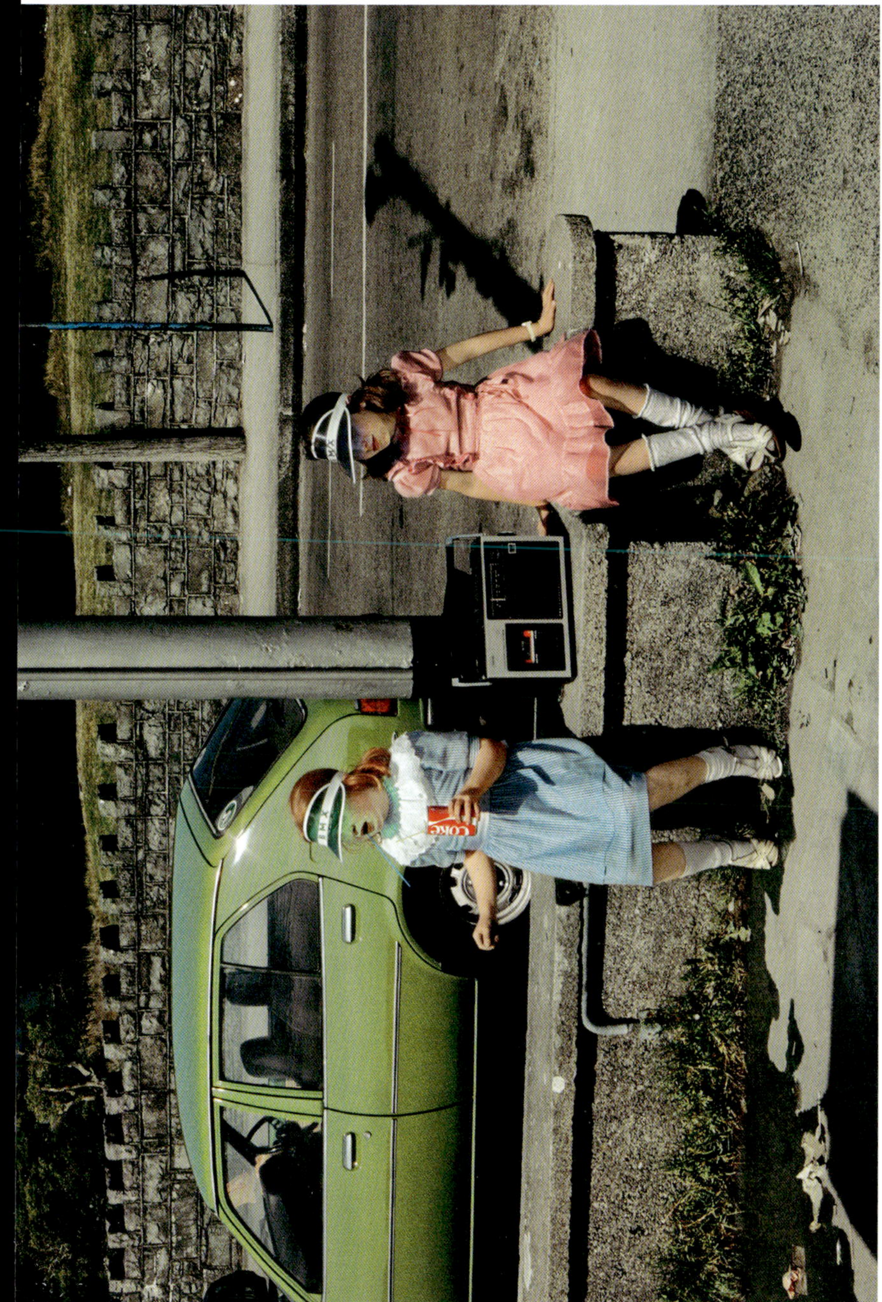

36. County Kerry, Ireland, 1984.

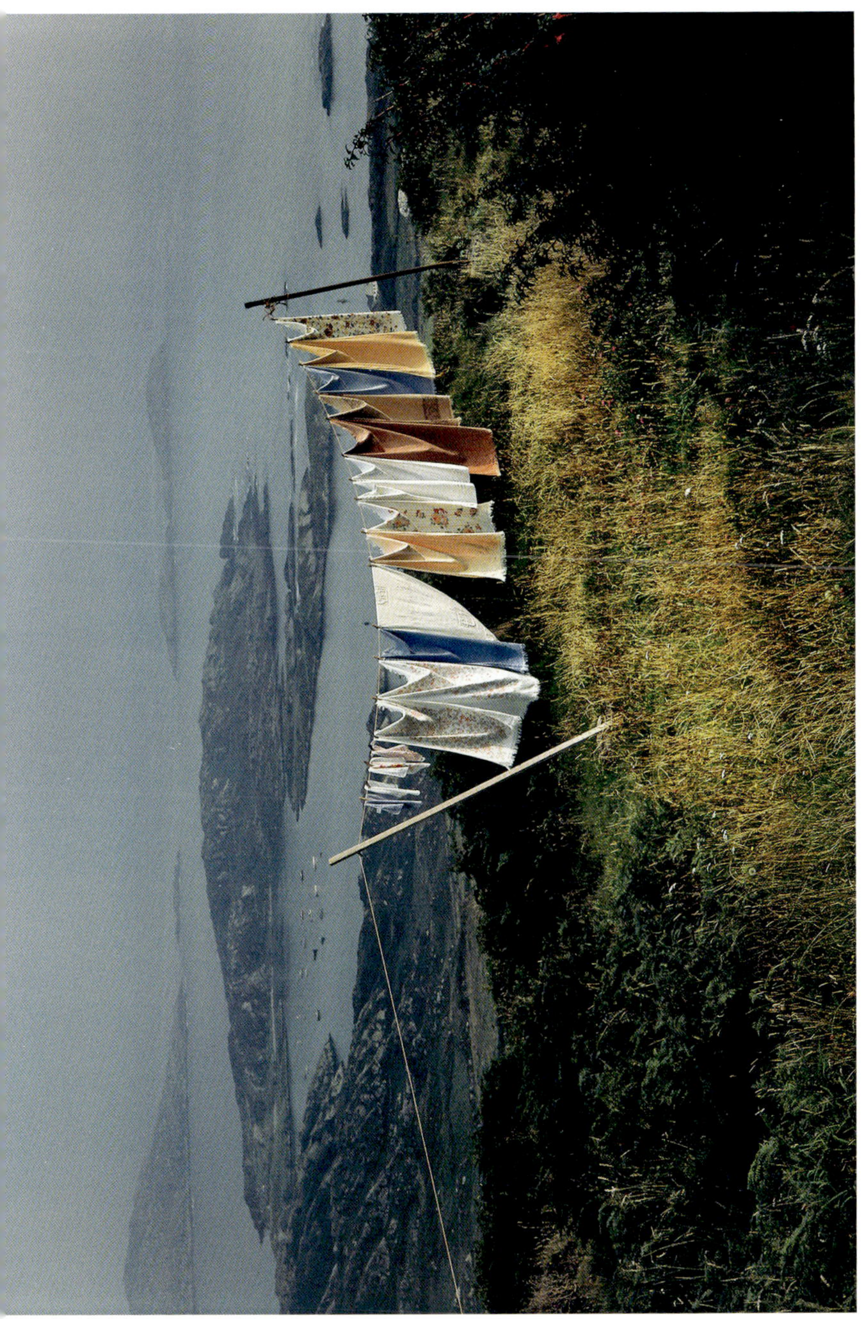

37. Baie des Anges, Nice, France, 1988.

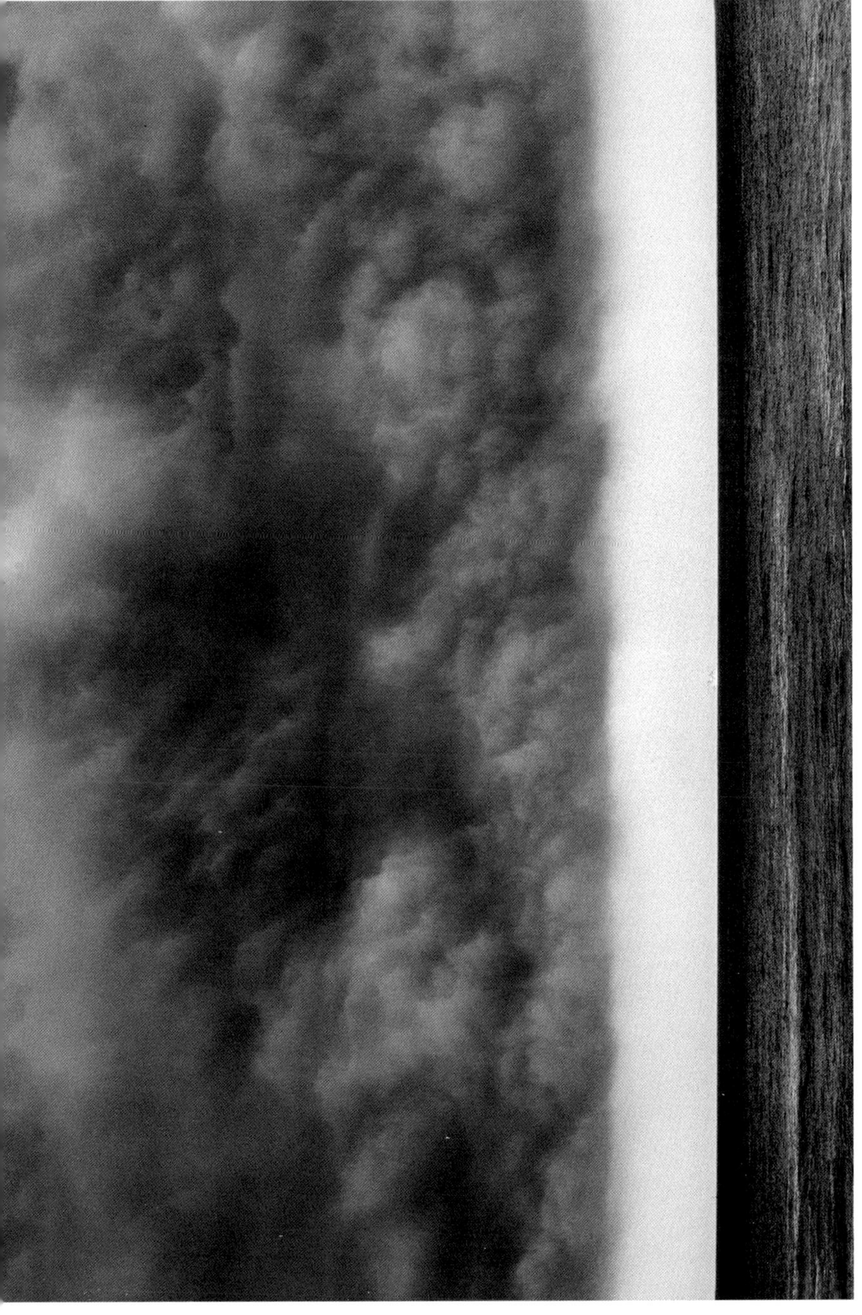

38. Ostend, Belgium, 1988.

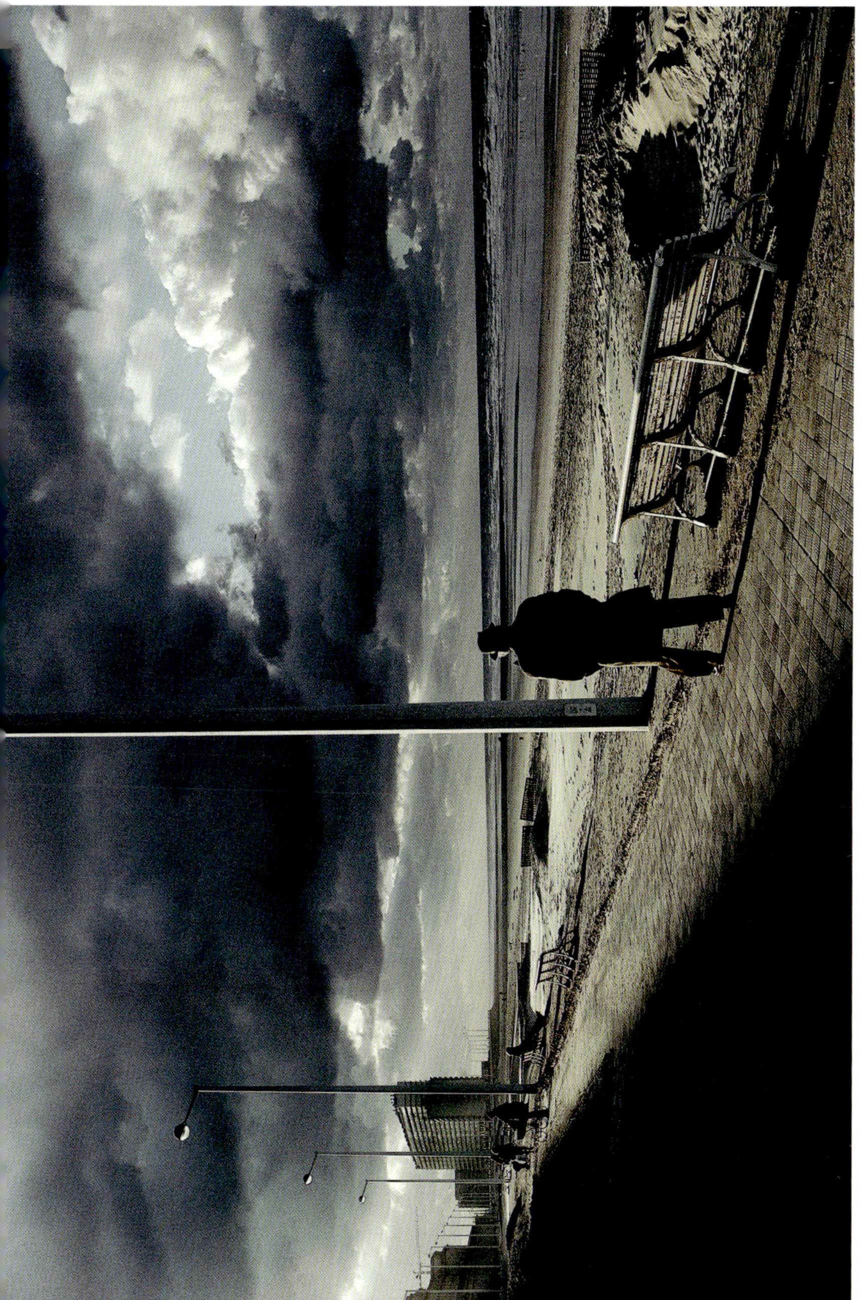

39. Fort-Mahon-Plage, France, 1991.

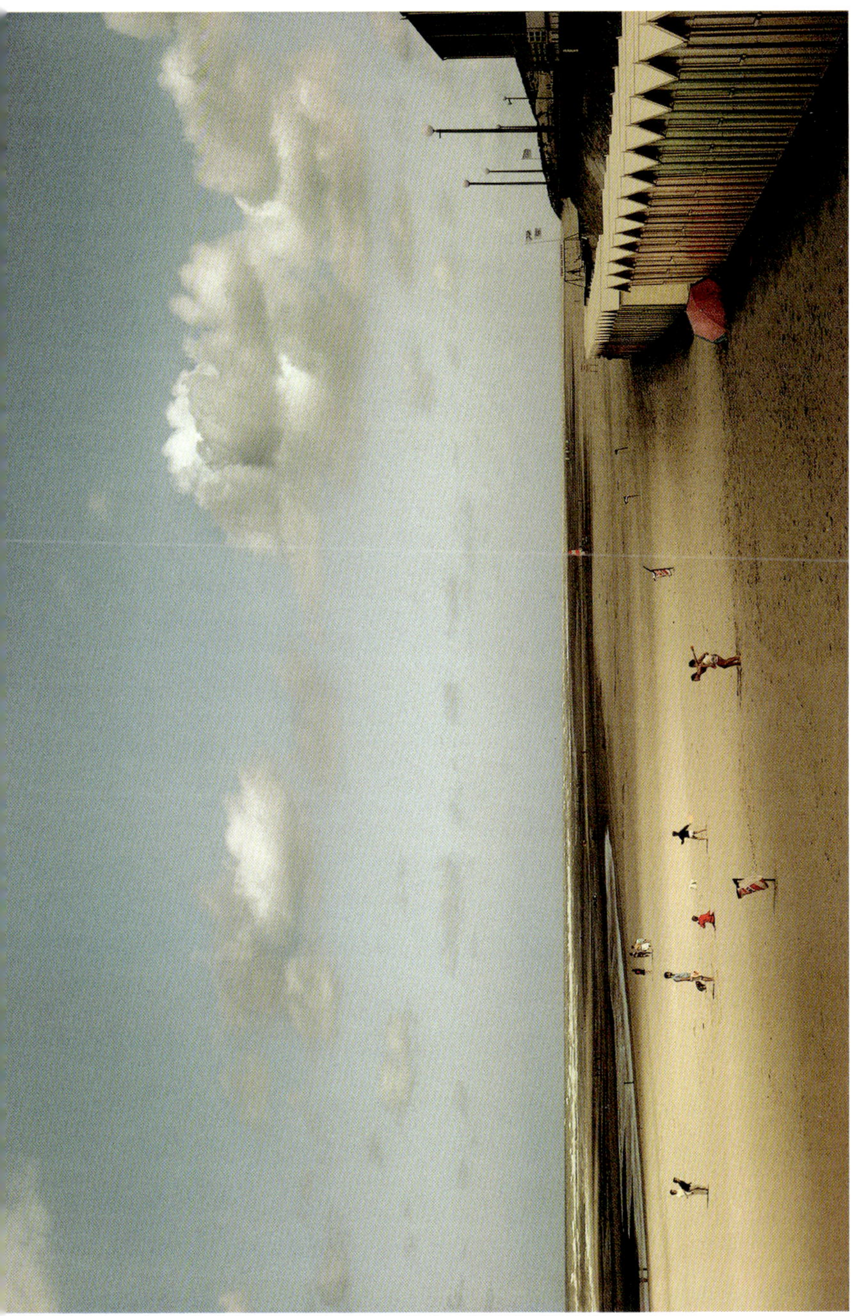

40. The river Niger, 1988.

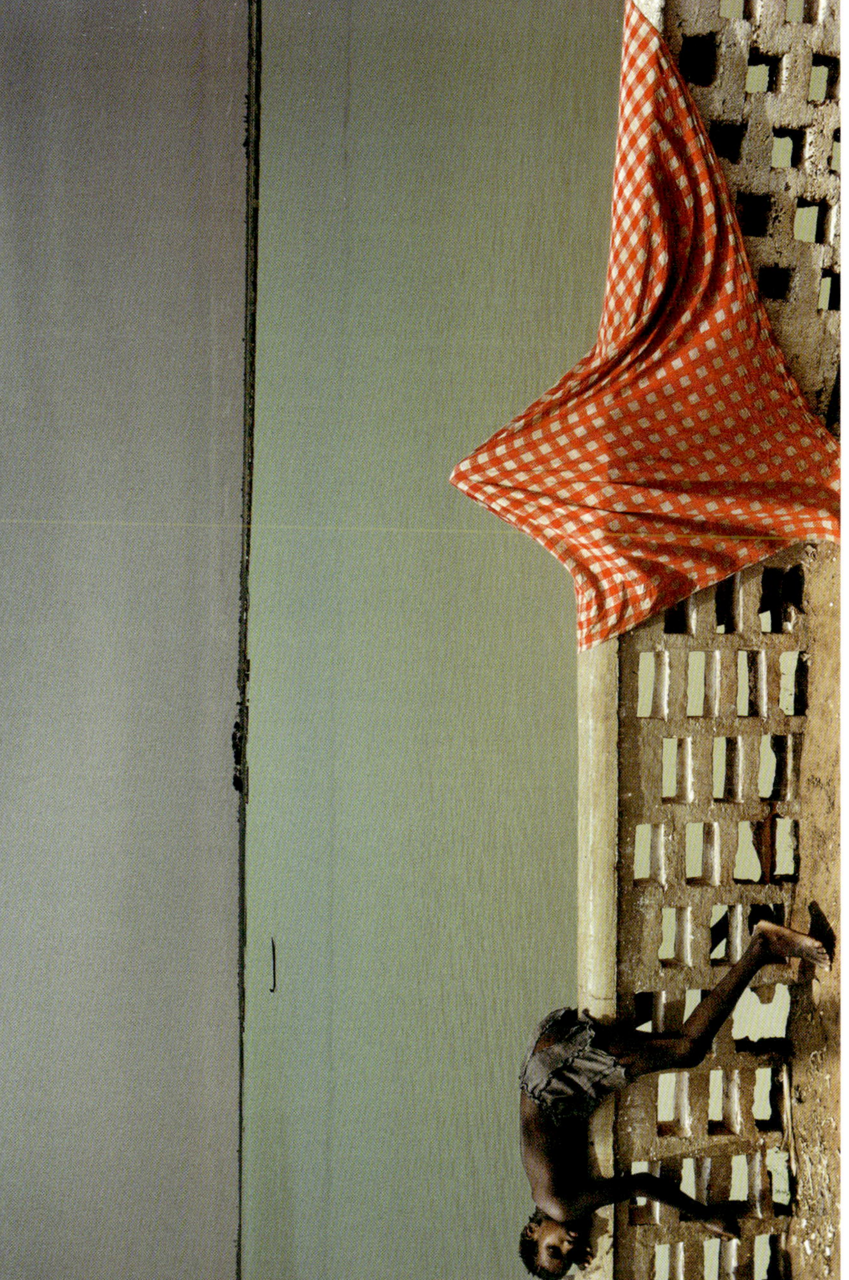

41. Gao, Mali, 1988.

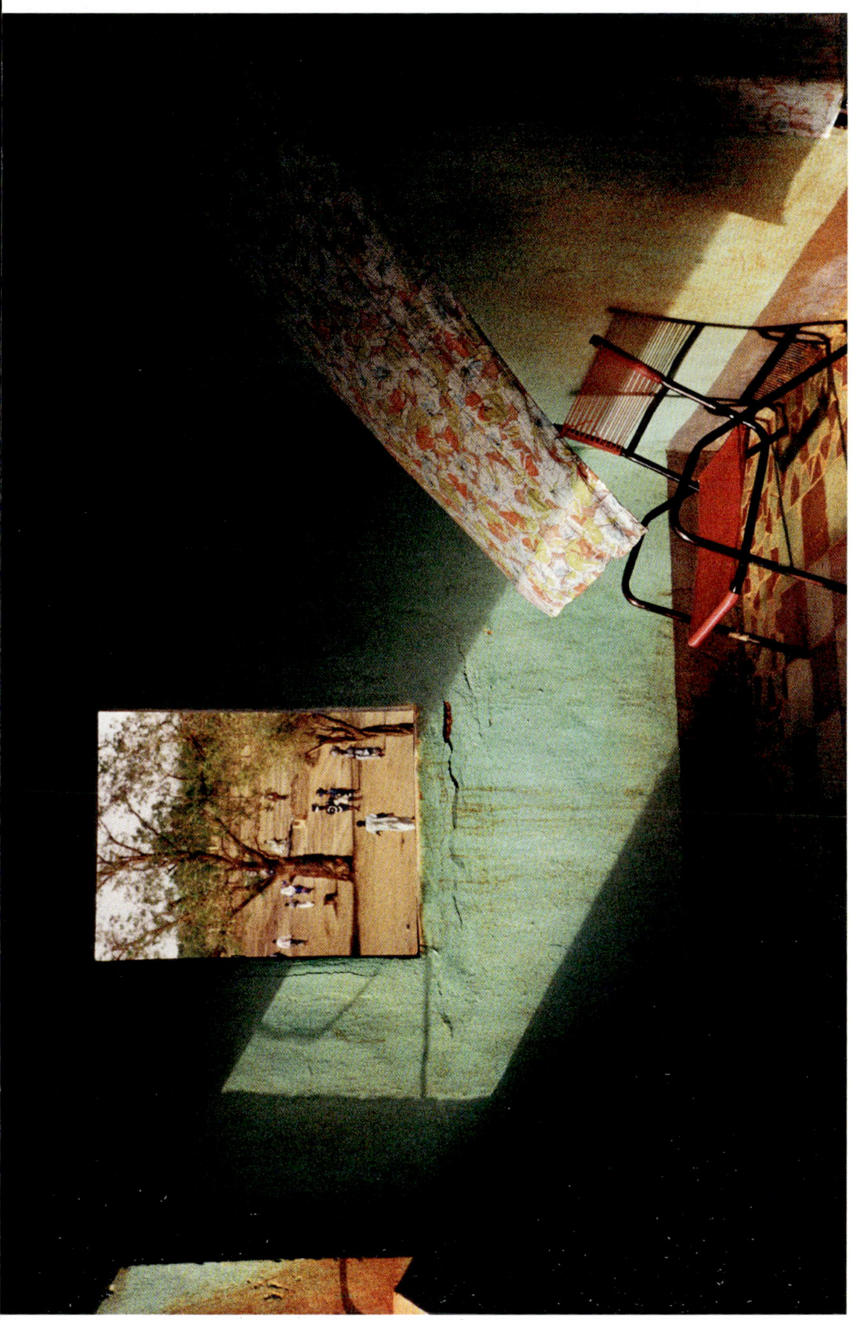

42. Asilah, Morocco, 1976

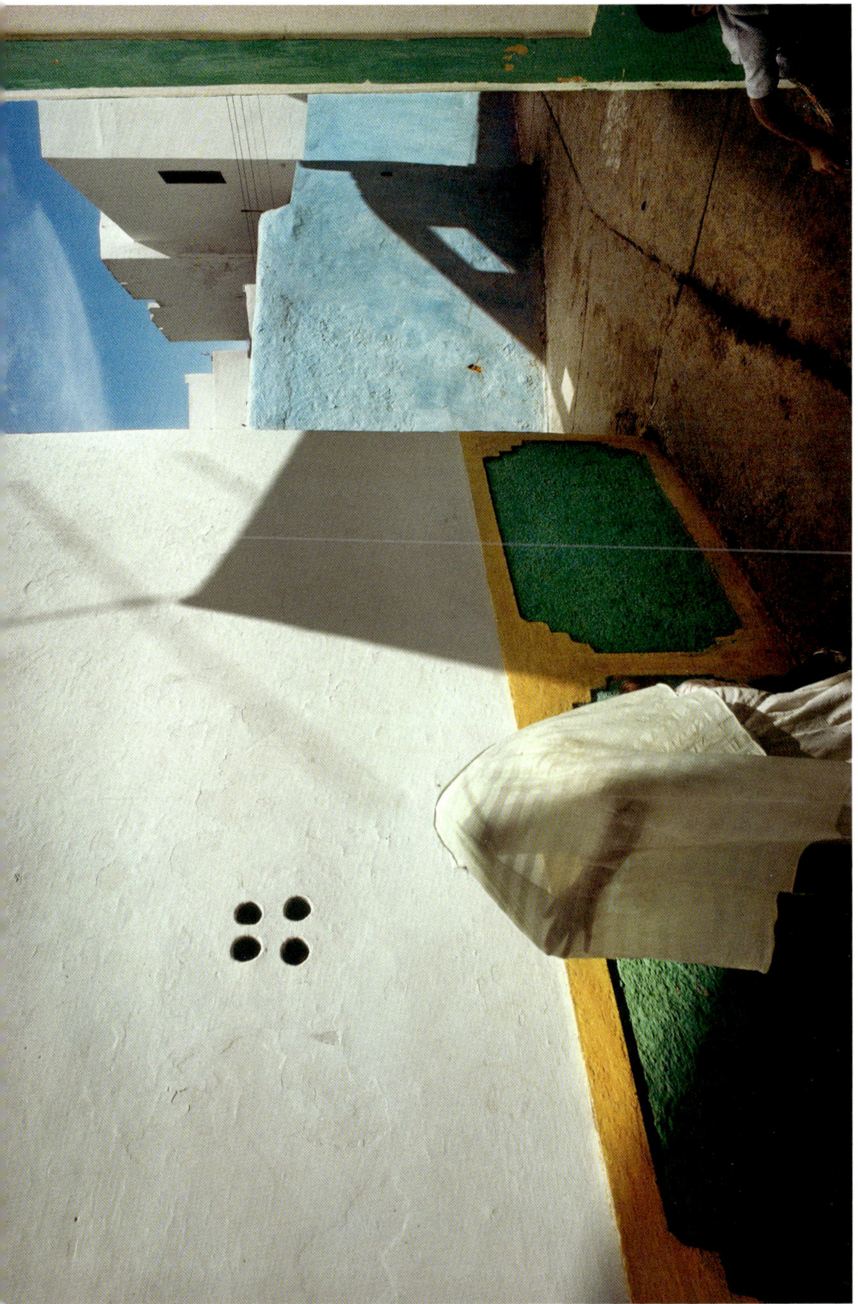

43. High Atlas mountains, 1998.

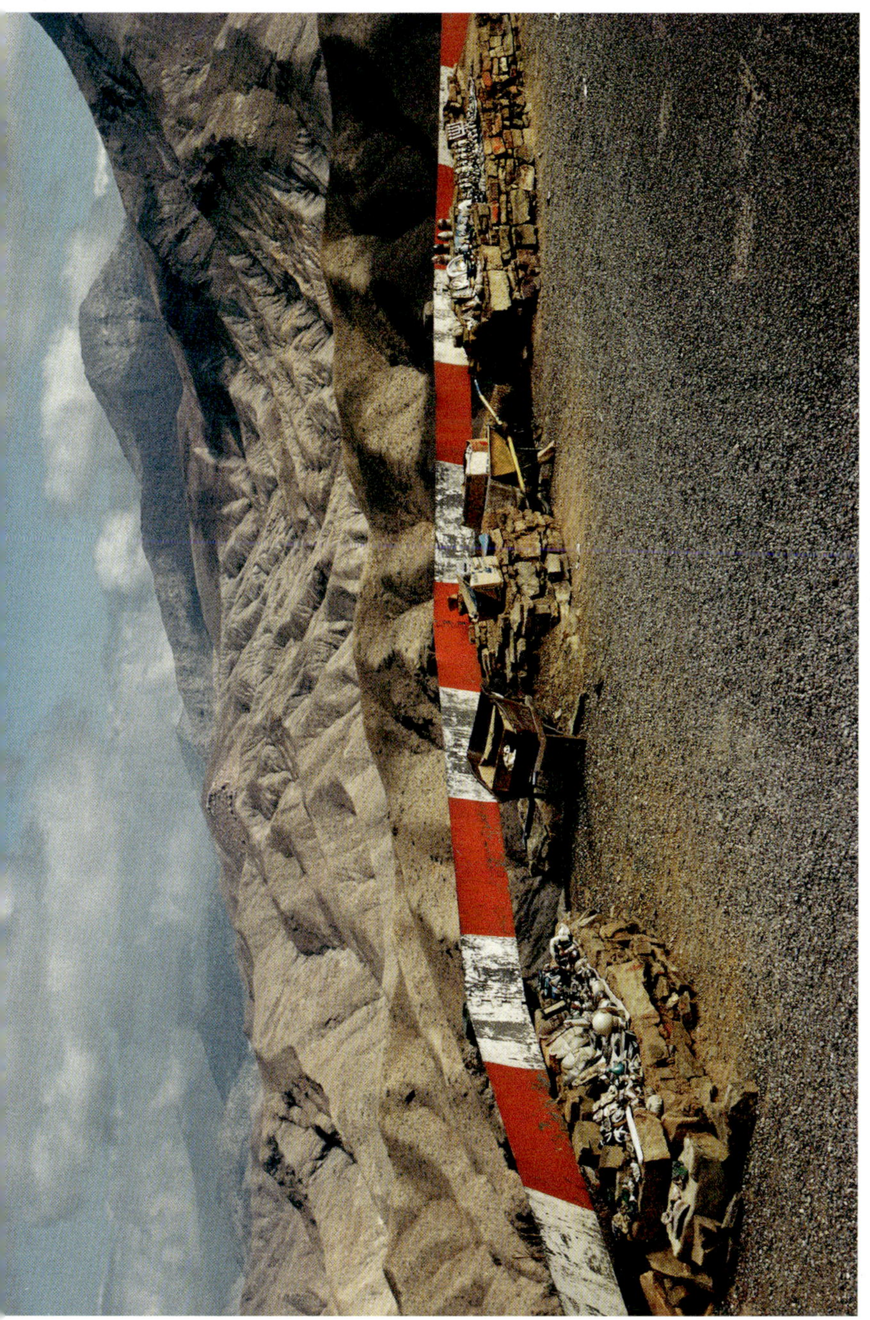

44. Cairo, Egypt, 1988.

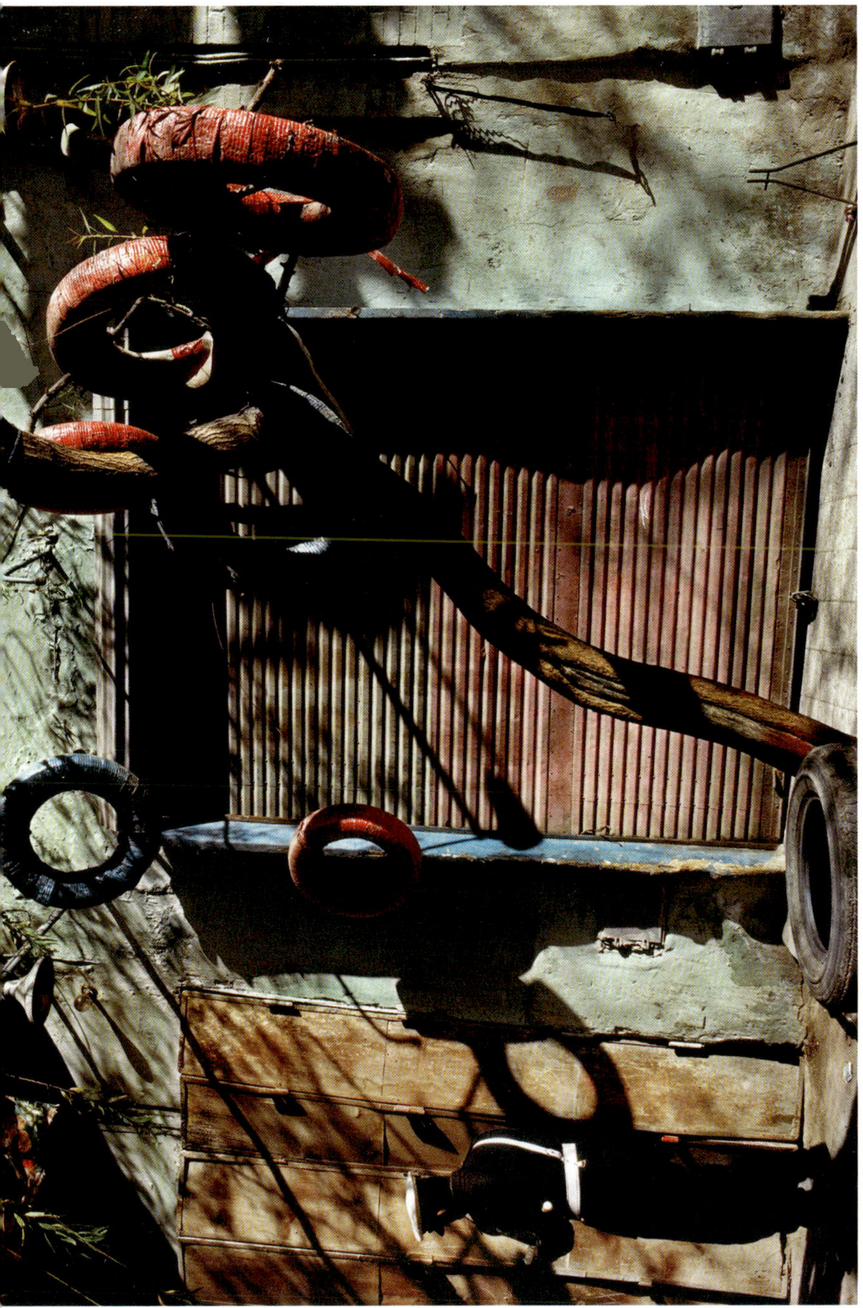

45. Old Delhi, India, 1985.

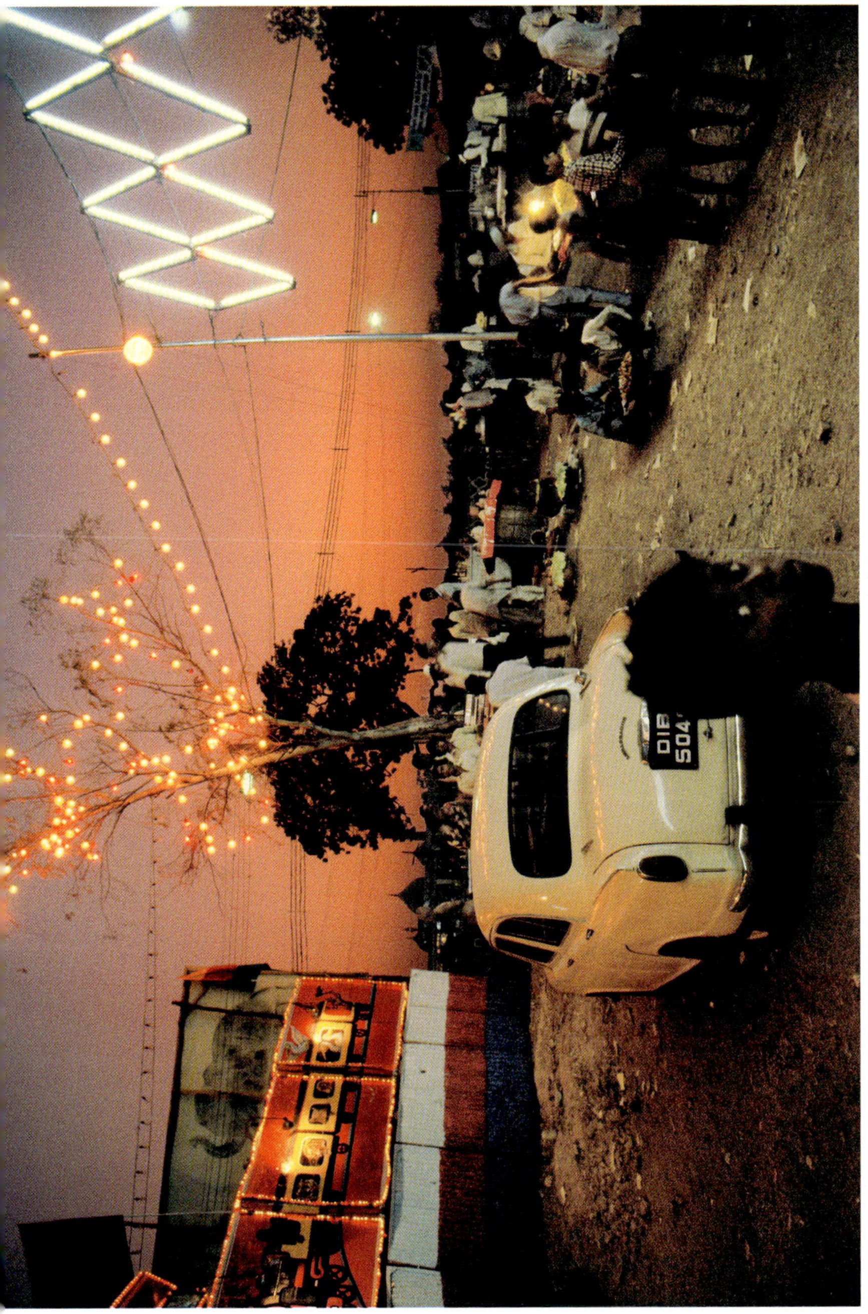

46. Ouarzazate, Morocco, 1986.

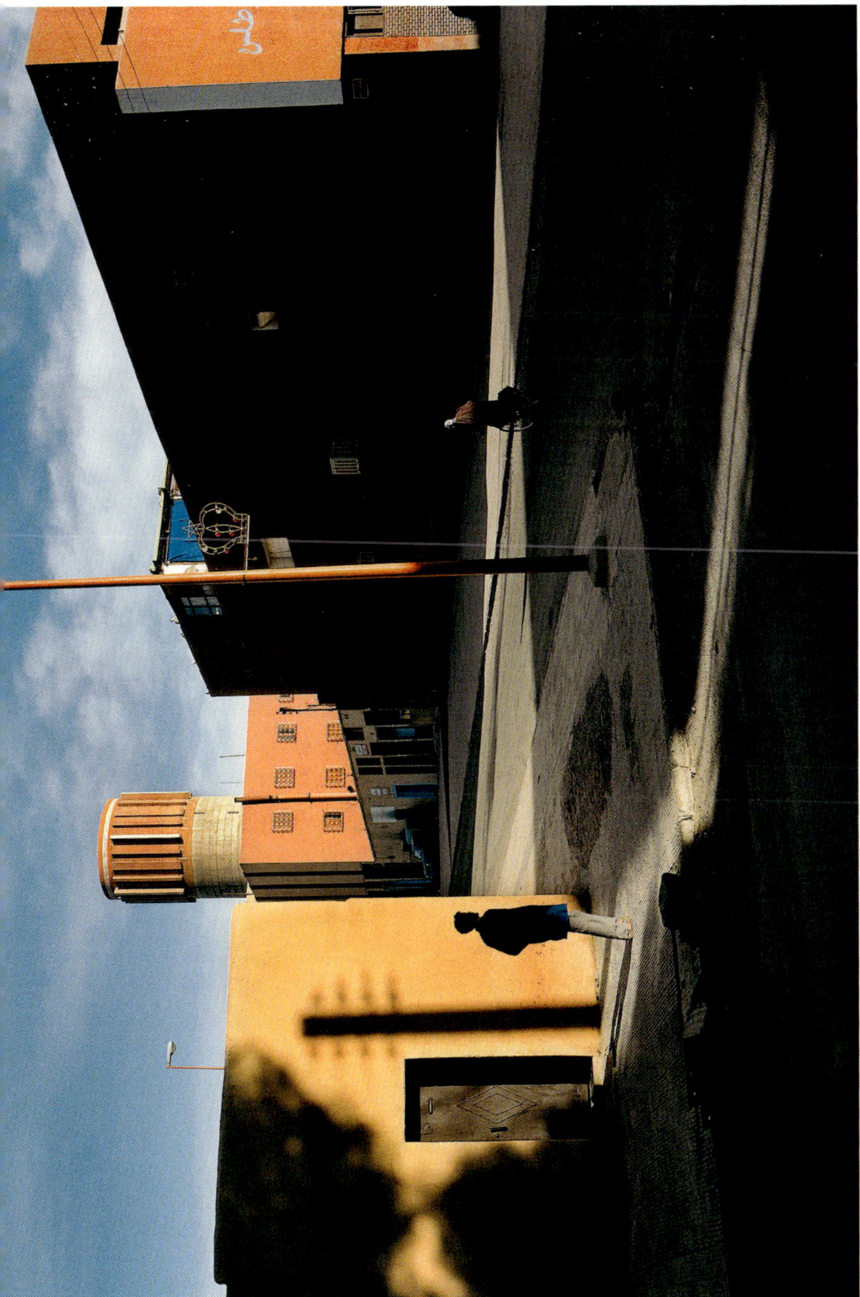

47. Erfoud, Morocco, 1986.

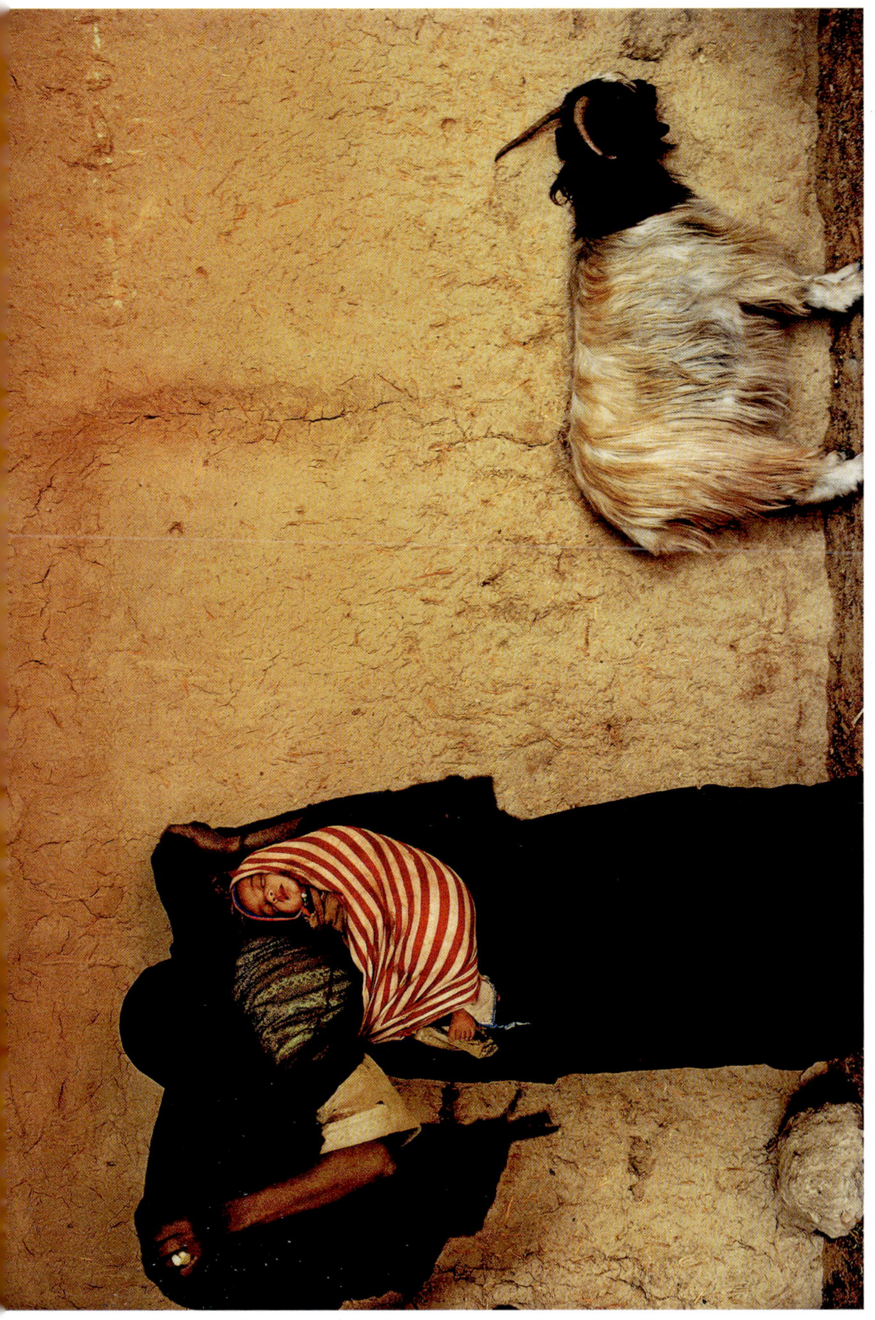

48. Jaisalmer, India, 1976.

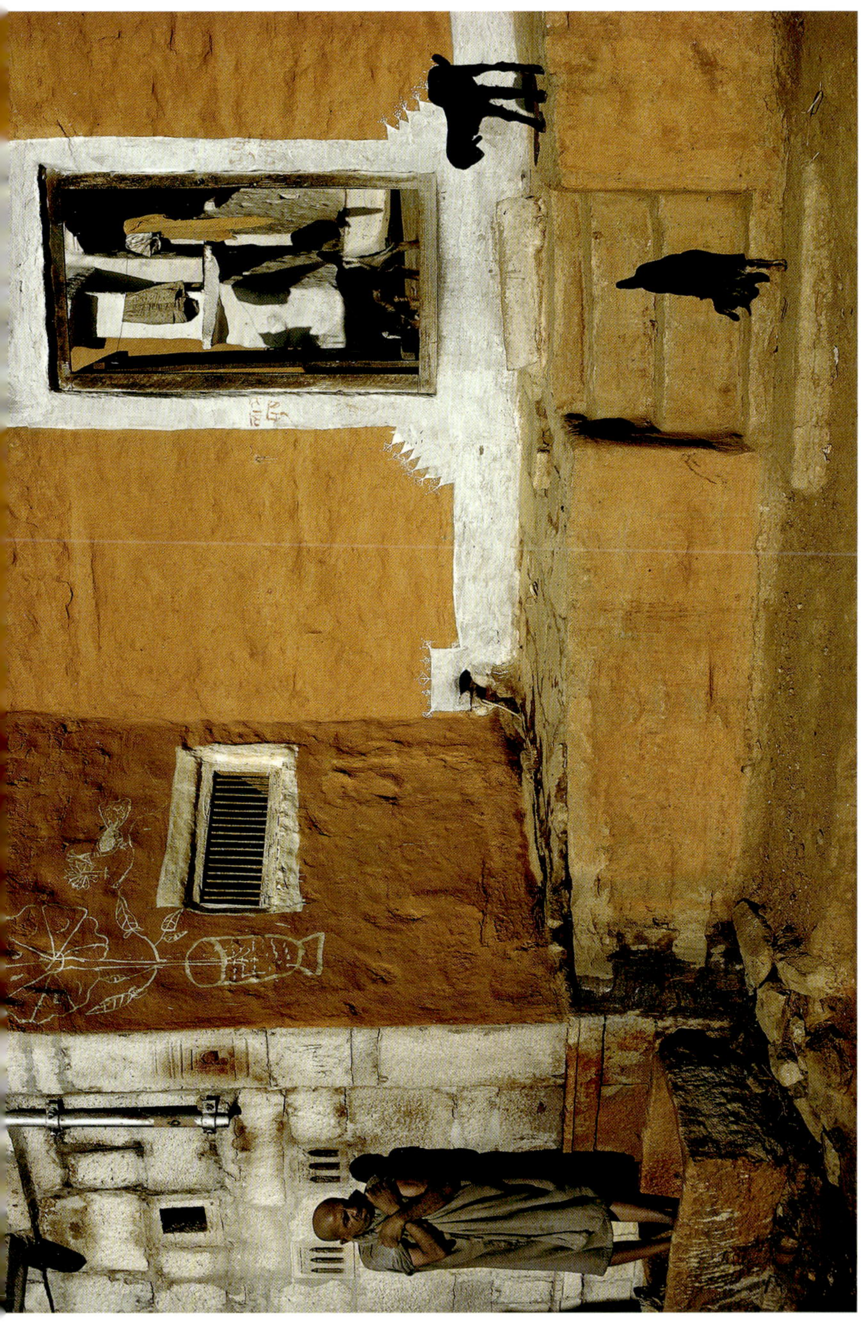

49. High Atlas mountains, 1986.

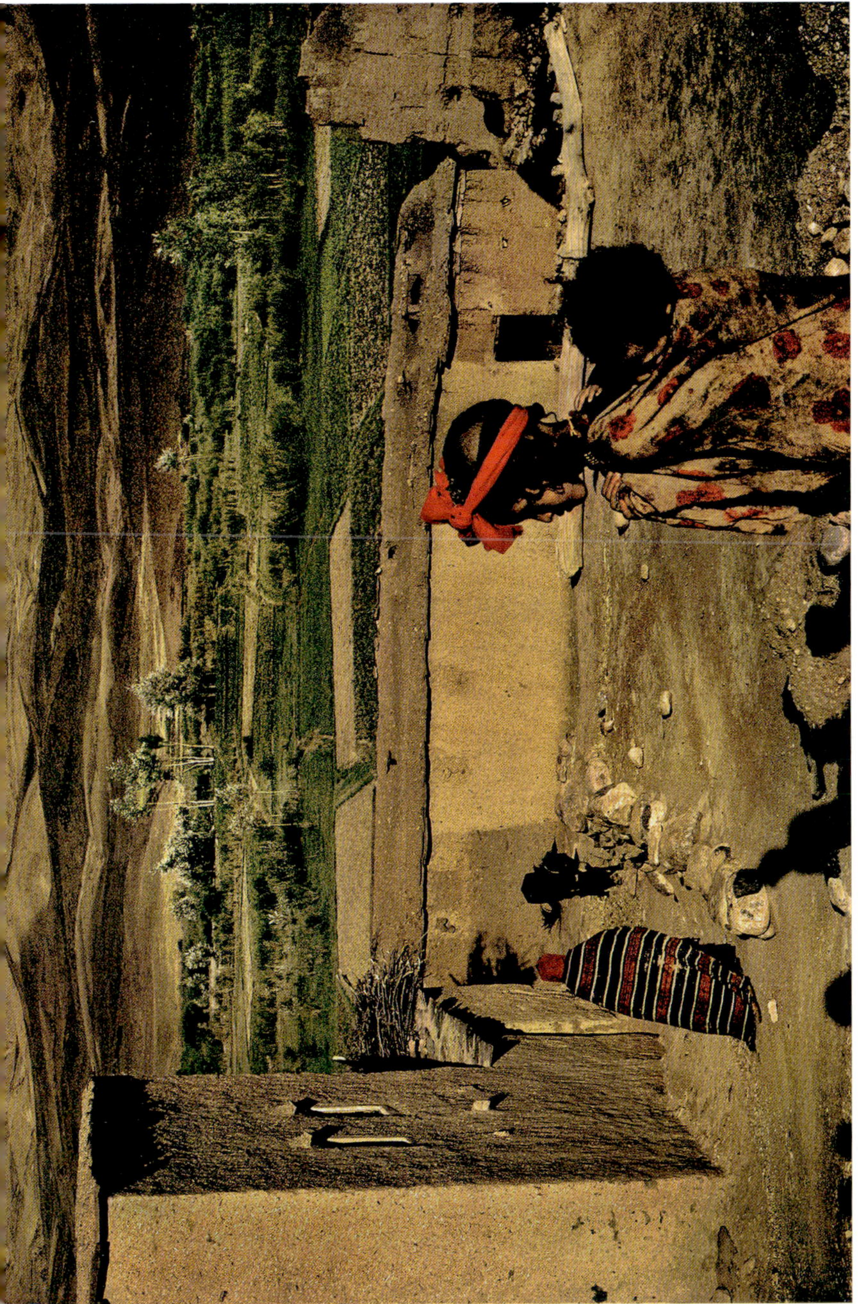

50. Essaouira, Morocco, 1988.

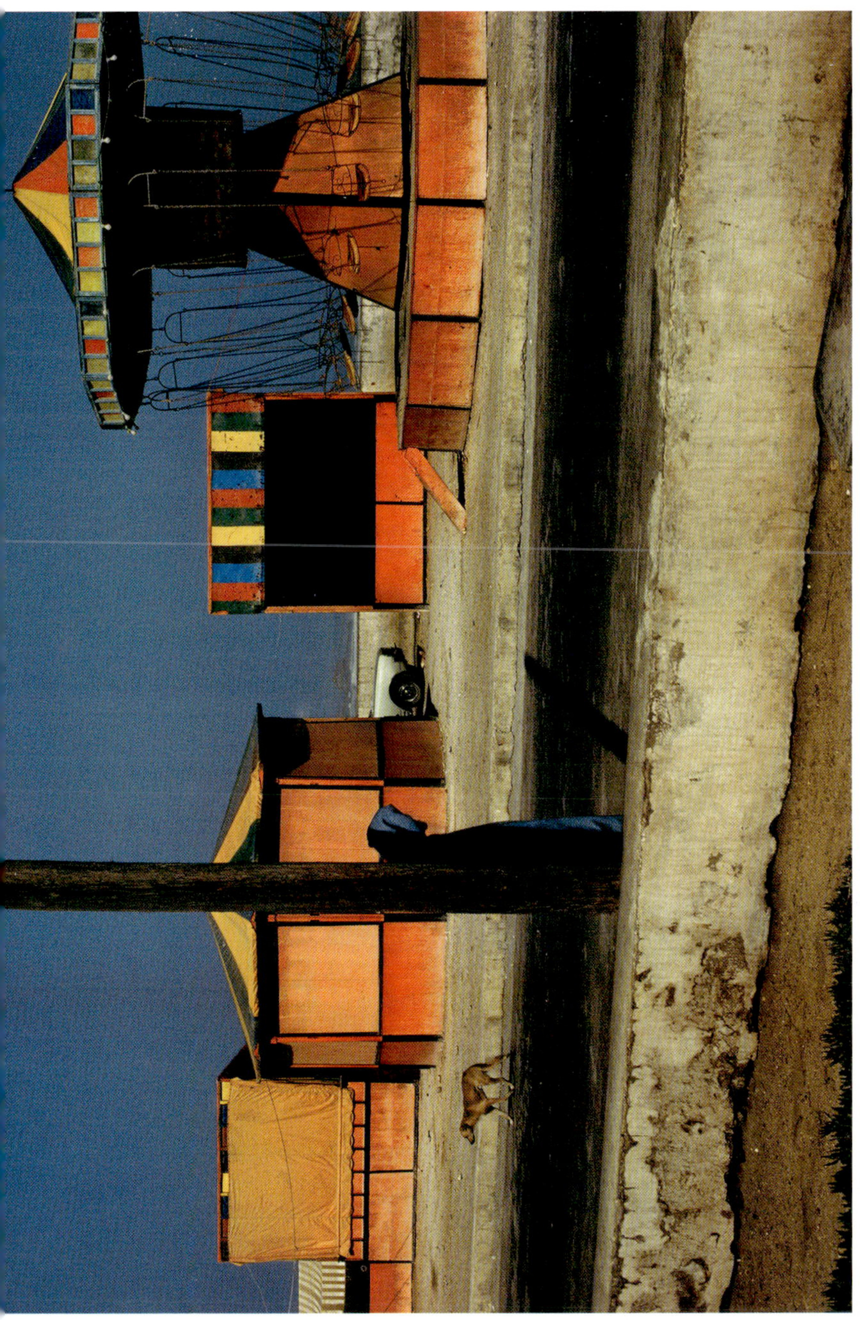

51. Thiruvananthapuram, India, 1989.

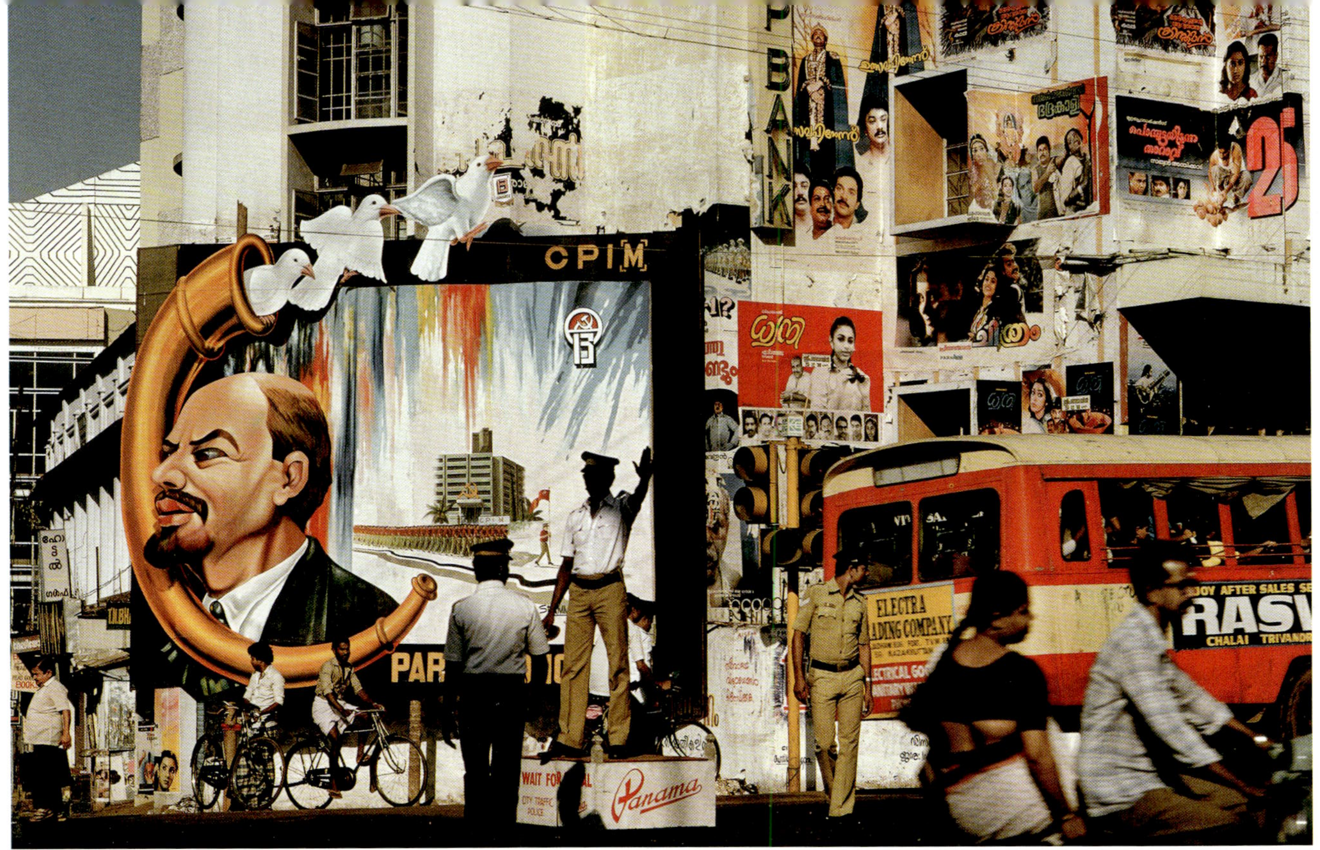
CPIM
BANK
25
RASW
ENJOY AFTER SALES SE
CHALAI TRIVANDR
ELECTRA
ADING COMPANY
ELECTRICAL GO
Panama
WAIT FOR
CITY TRAFFIC
POLICE
PAR

52. Marrakech, Morocco, 1988.

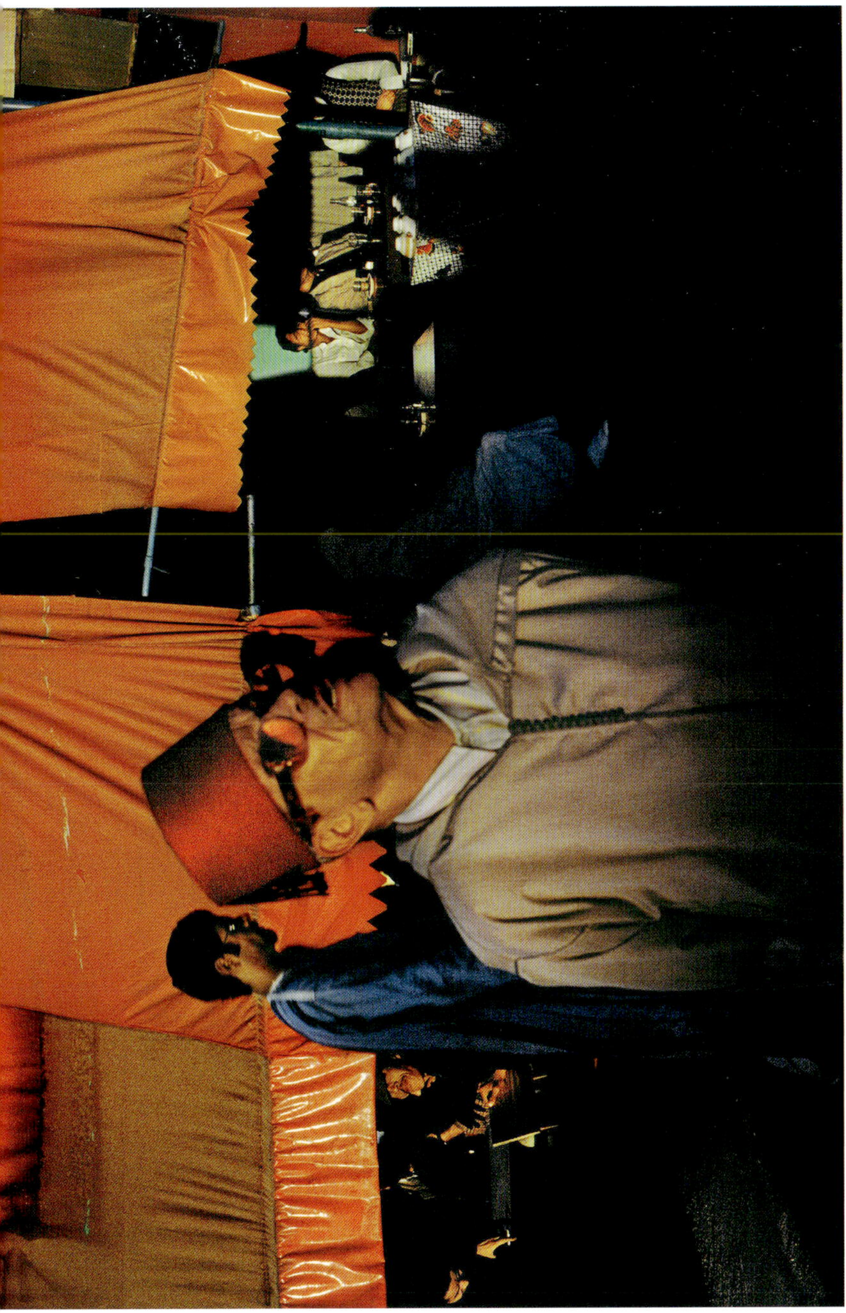

53. Marrakech, Morocco, 1986.

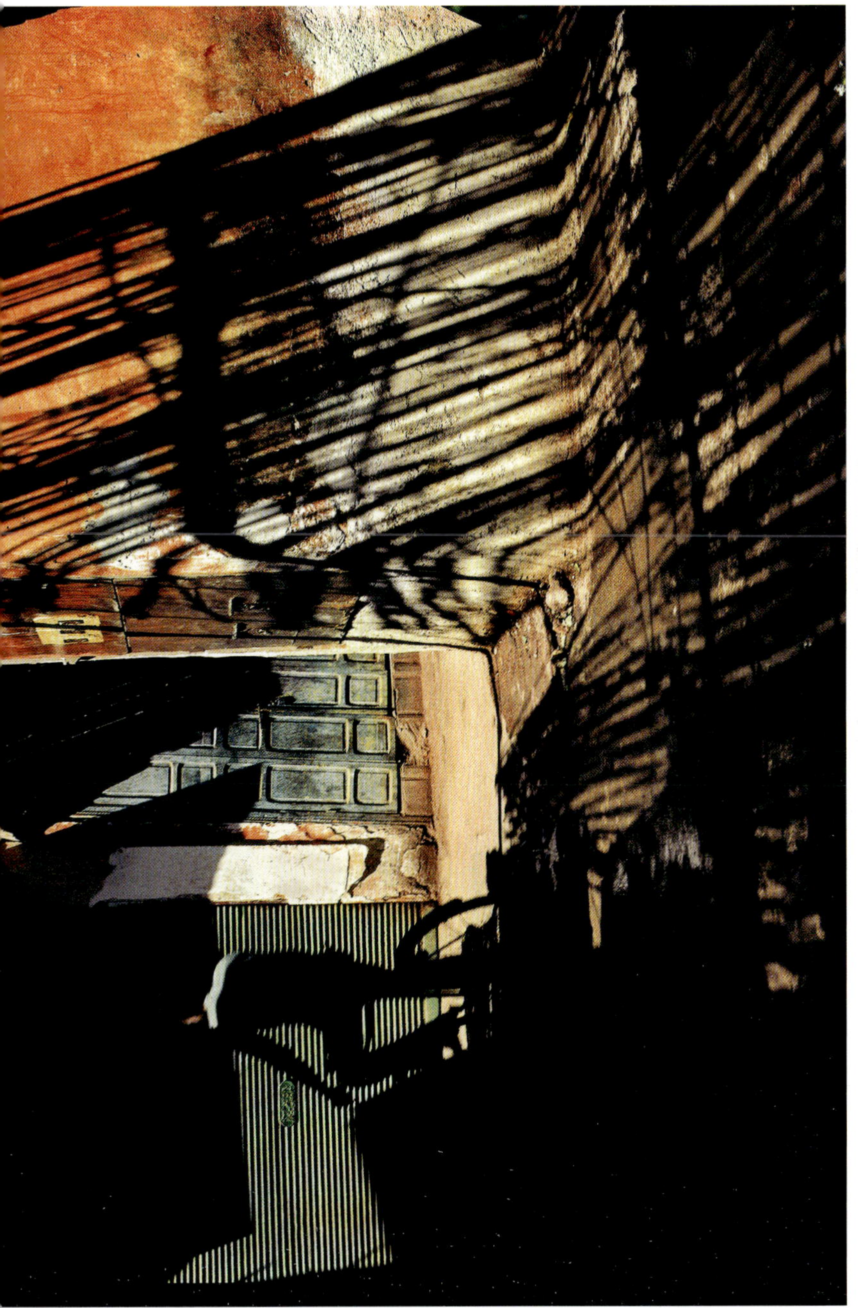

54. Cochin, India, 1989.

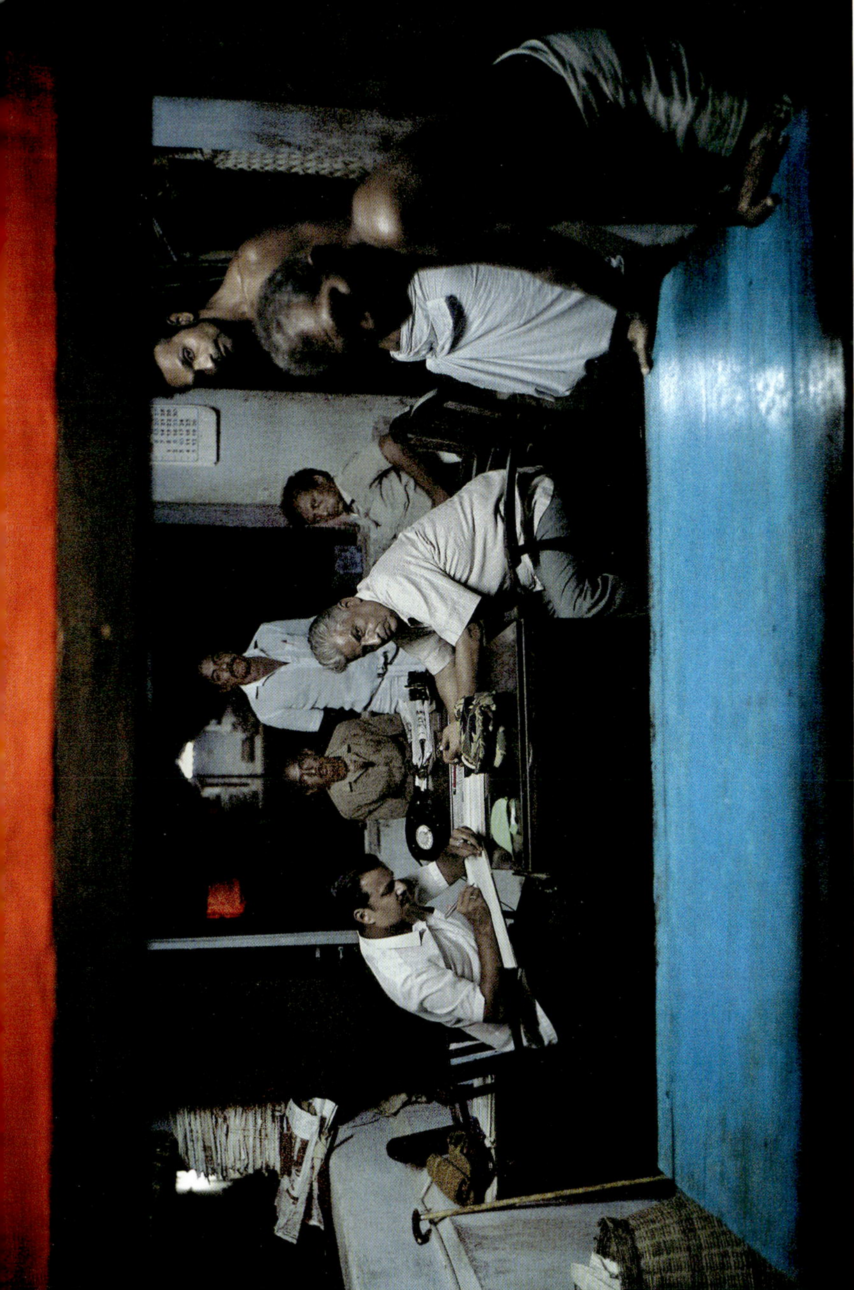

55. Las Vegas airport, 1982.

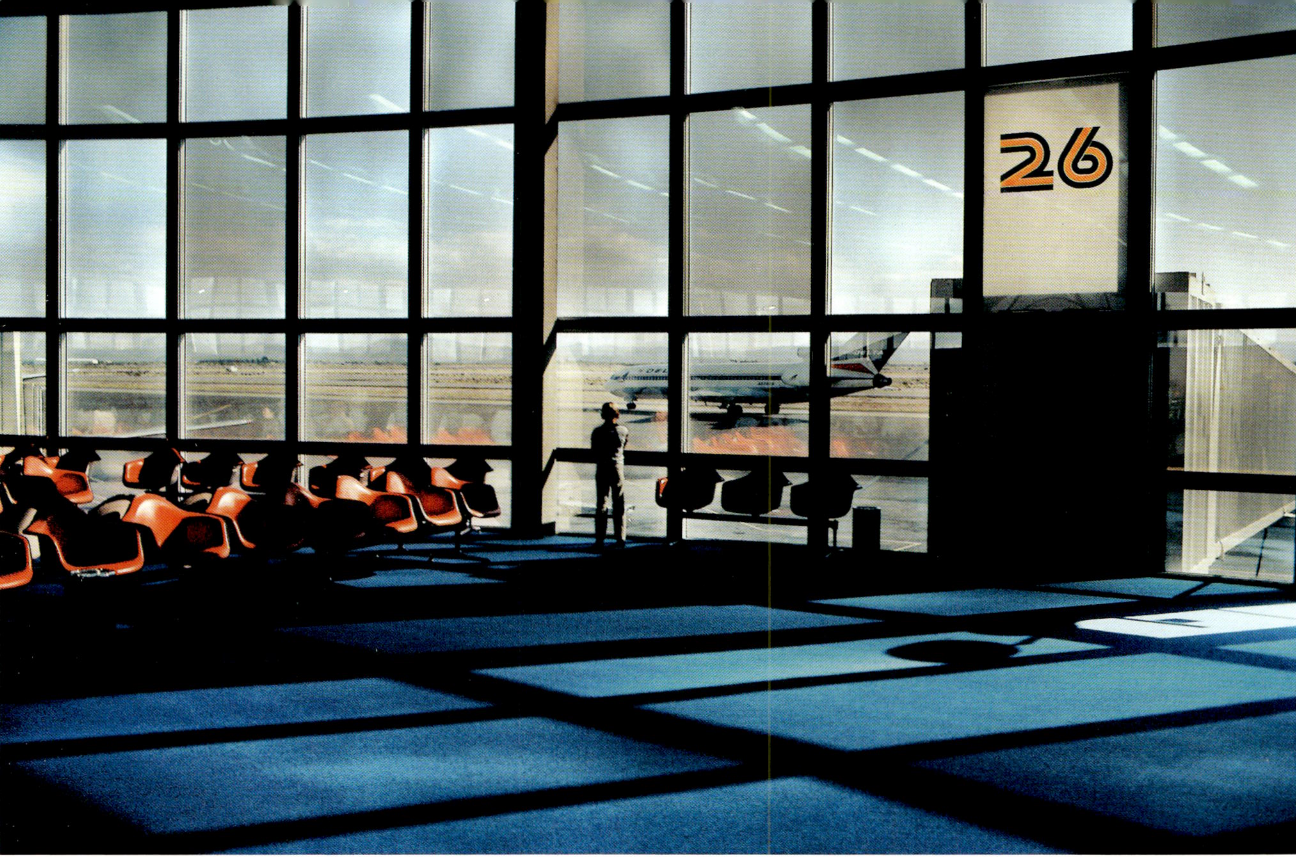
26

56. Entrance of GUM department store, Moscow, 1989.

Overleaf:
57. Istanbul, 2006.
58. Shinjuku, Tokyo, 1996.

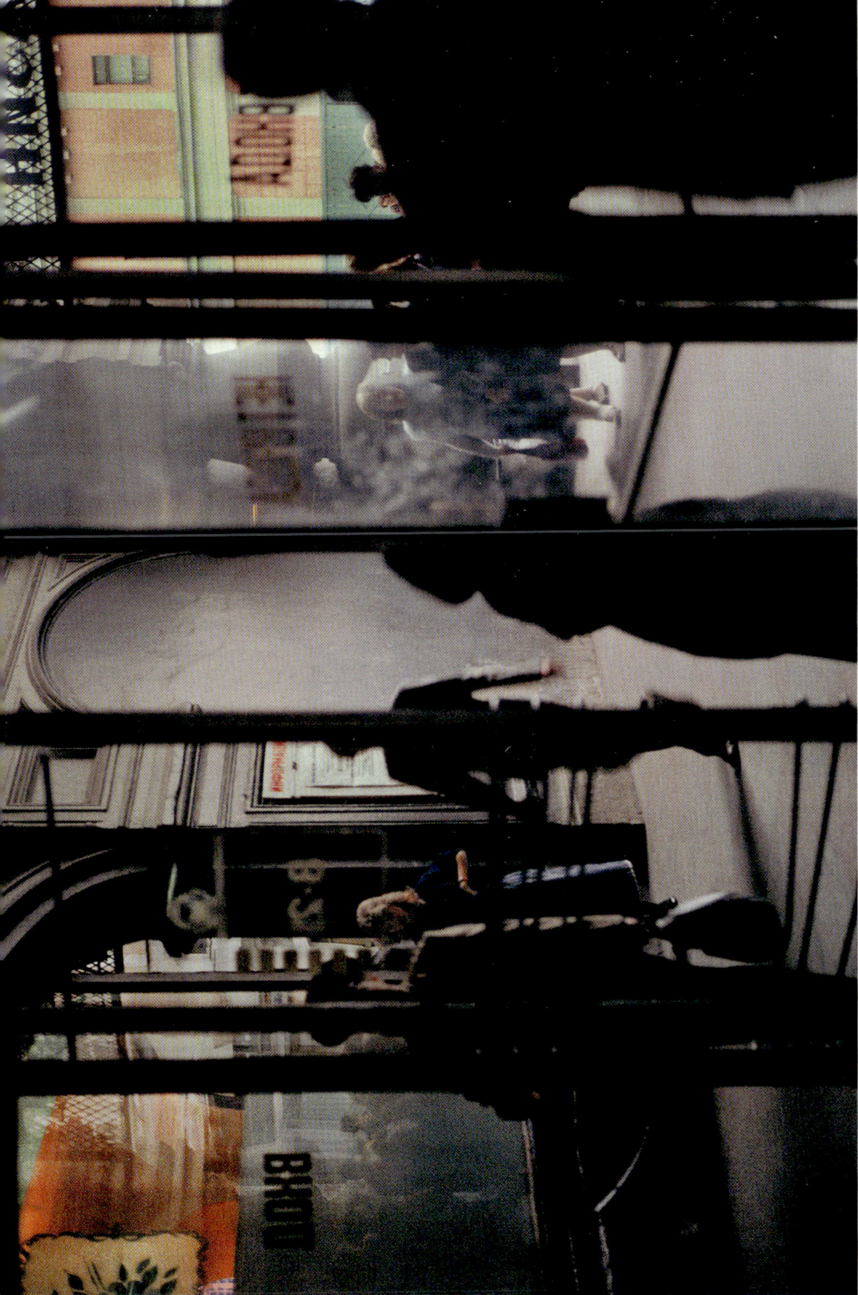

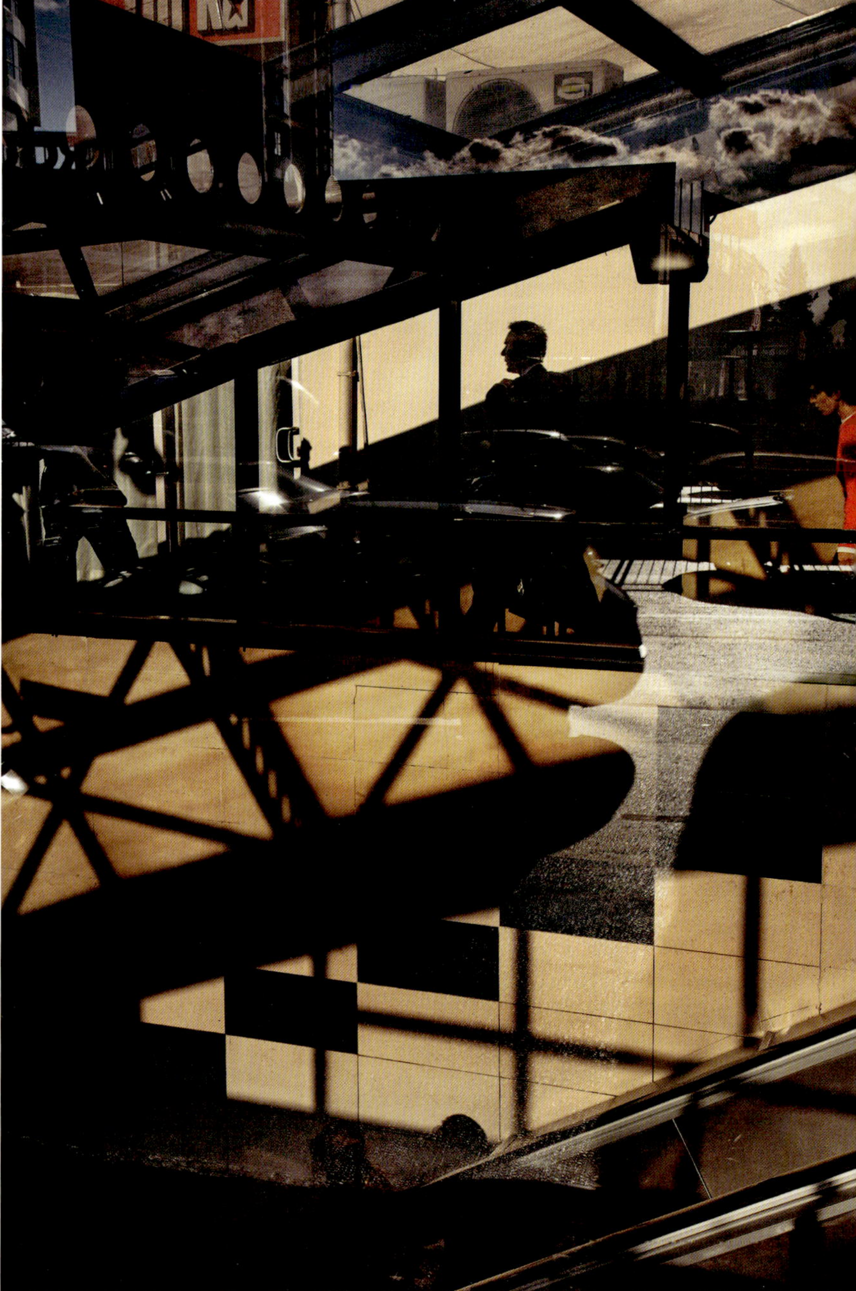

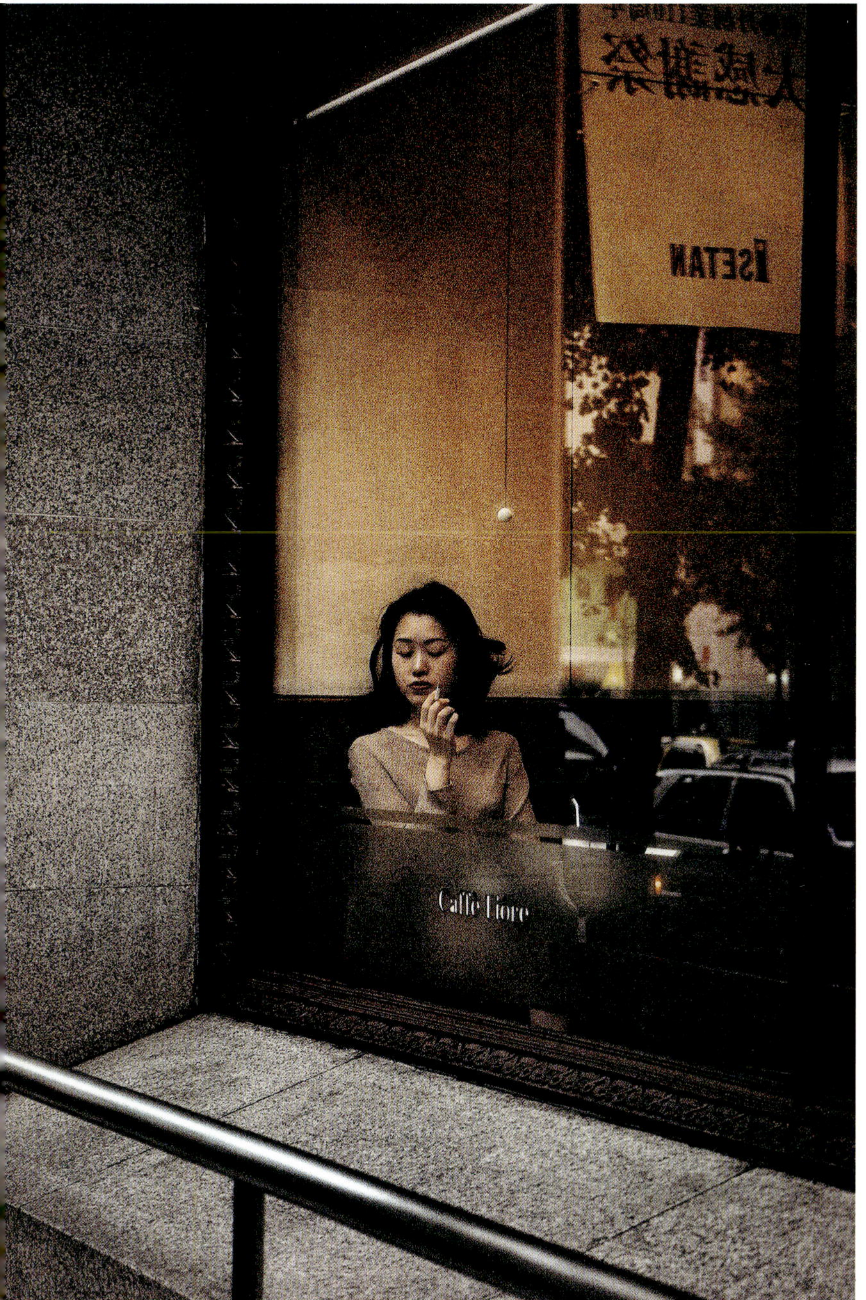
ISETAN
Caffè Fiore

59. New York, 1985.

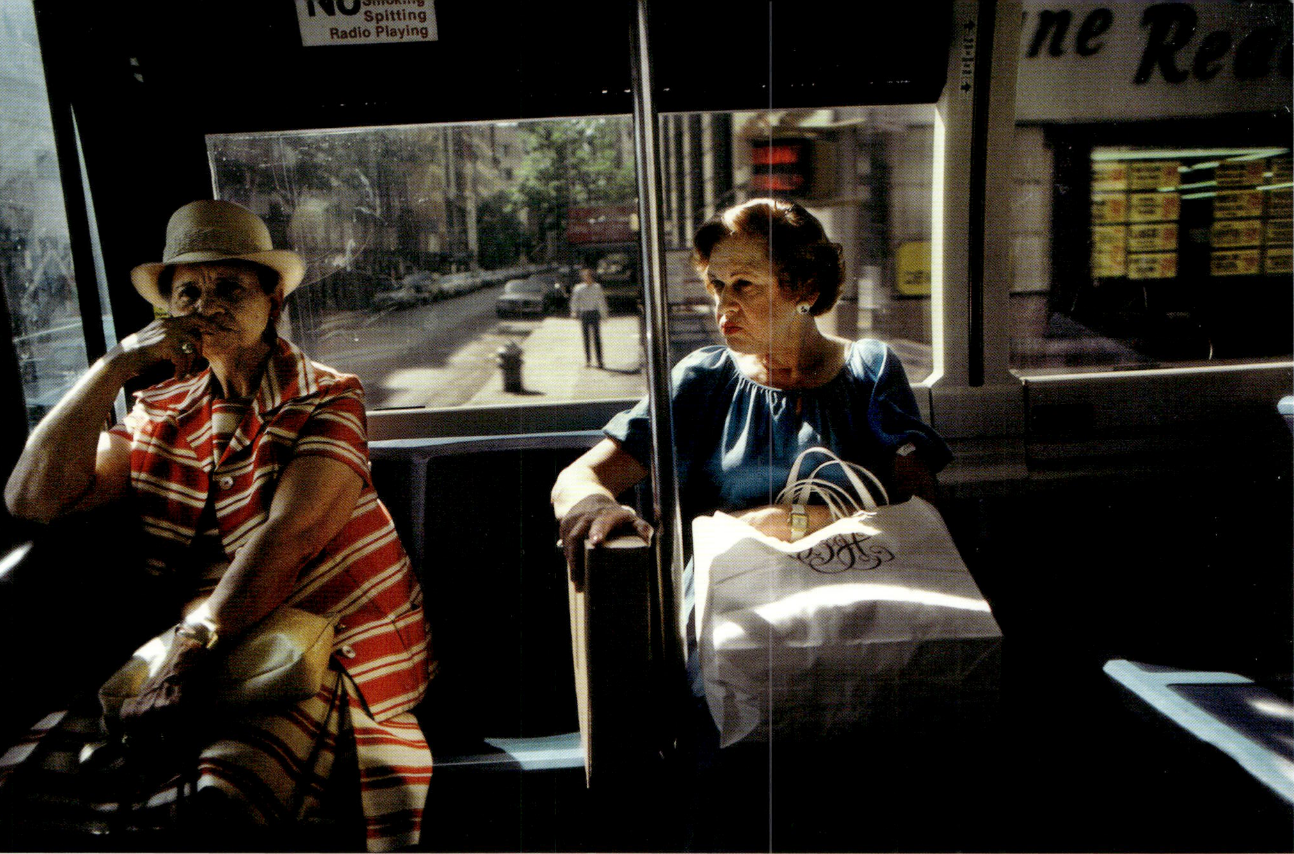
NO Smoking
Spitting
Radio Playing
ne Red

60. Moscow, 1989.

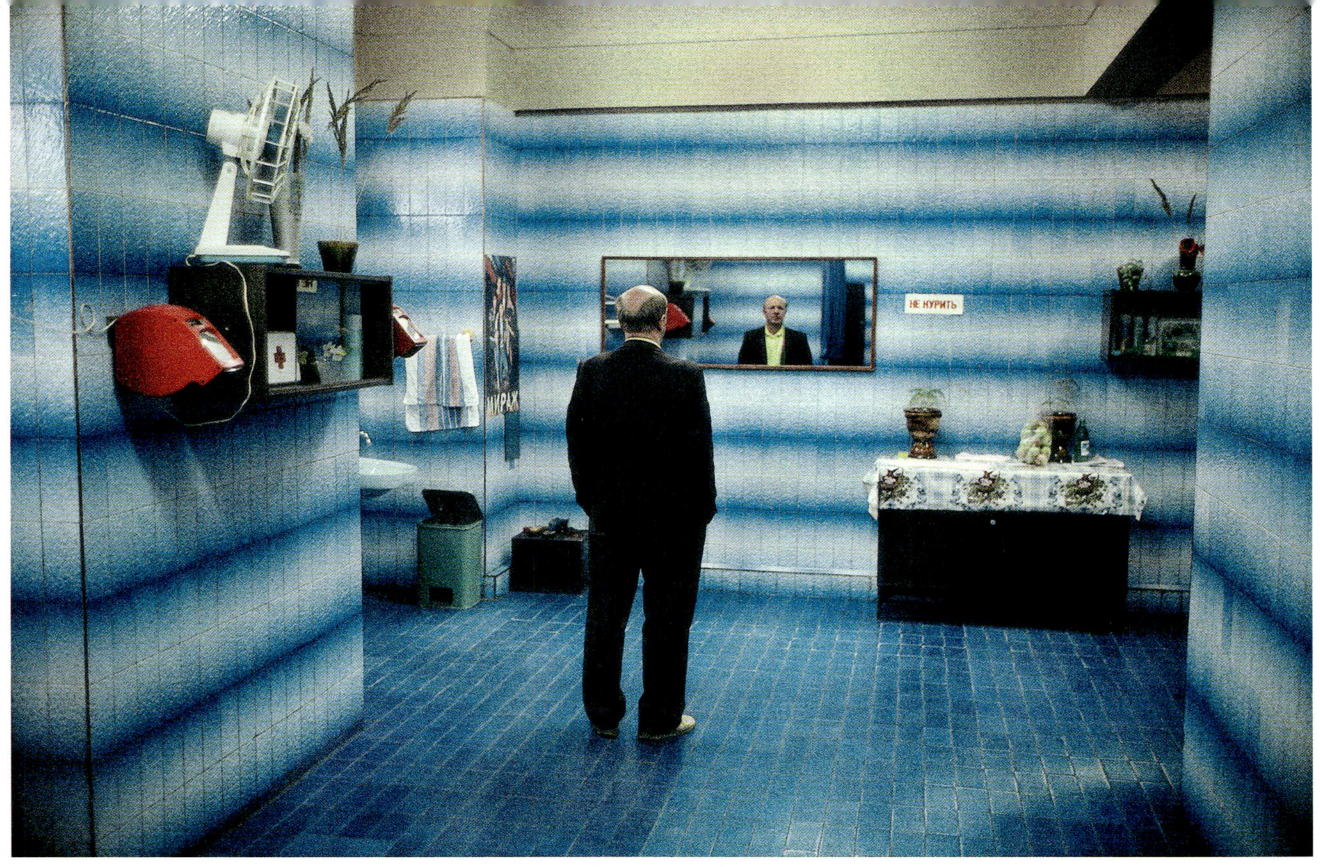
МИРАЖ
НЕ КУРИТЬ

61. Bal du Rat Mort, Ostend, Belgium, 1988.

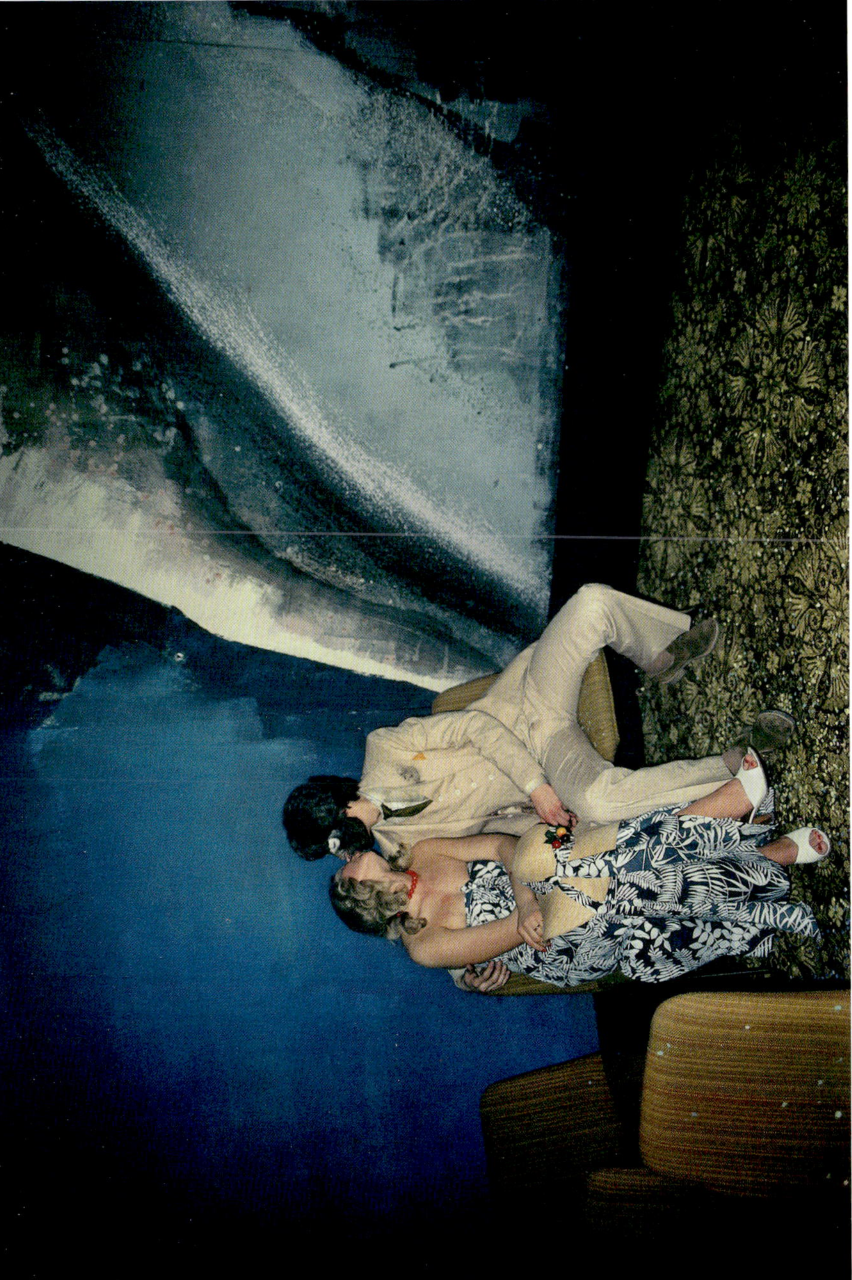

62. Antwerp, Belgium, 2008.

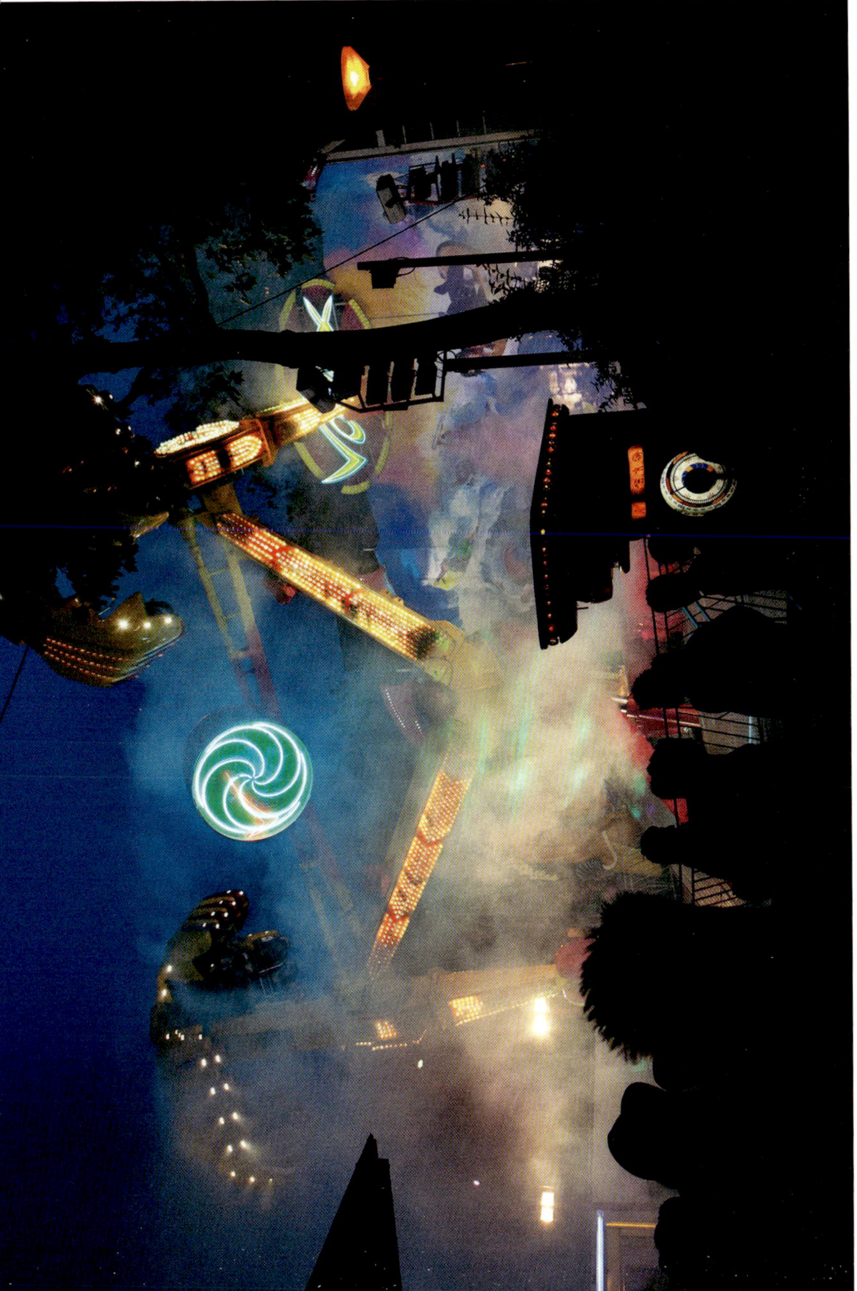

Biography

1941 Harry Gruyaert is born in Antwerp on 25 August.

1959–1962 Originally wanting to become a director, he studies film and photography in Brussels.

1963–1967 At the age of 21, he moves to Paris. There he meets the publisher and gallery owner Robert Delpire, who several years later will exhibit and publish his work. He begins to photograph the capital and also works as a director of photography on documentaries by Belgian director Jef Cornelis.

1968 He travels to the USA for the first time and discovers Pop artists including Roy Lichtenstein and Robert Rauschenberg. These new influences lead to a growing interest in the creative potential of colour and the beauty of banality. He befriends American artists Gordon Matta-Clark and Richard Nonas. The latter will go on to write forewords for several of his books.

1969 He visits Morocco for the first time, a country that will leave its mark on him, and where he will take many photographs. These will be later published in two books, *Morocco* (1990) and *Maroc* (2013).

1971 He moves to London.

1972 He photographs the Munich Olympics and the early Apollo flights in colour, from the screen of a detuned television set. These images become the basis for the series *TV Shots*, which will be the subject of a book (2007) and will join the collection of the Centre Pompidou.

1973 He returns to Paris and begins a long photography project on Belgium, the land of his birth. This series will be published in the books *Made in Belgium* (2000) and *Roots* (2012 & 2018).

1976 He wins the Kodak Prize for his images of Morocco. He visits the exhibition *William Eggleston's Guide* at MoMA and discovers dye-transfer, a printing technique that gives colour great sensuality.

He travels to India for the first time and shoots a new series of images, which later become the book *India* (2020).

1981 He is invited to join Magnum Photos, during a period when he is one of the few photographers working in colour. Four years later, he becomes a full member of Magnum and a shareholder.

1984 He receives a research and creativity grant from the French Ministry of Culture to continue his work on India.

1987 He visits Egypt. Over the next few years, he travels across Asia, the USA, the Middle East and Africa.

1989 Just before the fall of the Berlin Wall, he visits Moscow with fellow photographer Josef Koudelka. His images of the city will later be published in the book *East/West* (2017).

2000 With Kodachrome film soon to be discontinued, he gives up analogue photography in favour of digital. Very exacting about the quality of his prints, formerly done with Cibachrome and sometimes dye-transfer, he experiments with inkjet printing in order to obtain the level of precision he demands.

2002 The exhibition *Jours de Fret*, a collaboration with Jean Gaumy, is held at the Rencontres de la Photographie d'Arles and accompanied by the publication of a book of the same name.

2003 The exhibition *Rivages* is held as part of the Rencontres de la Photographie d'Arles, and is accompanied by a book.

2004 A retrospective screening of his work is staged at the Théâtre Antique in Arles during the Rencontres de la Photographie festival.

2012 *Roots*, a collection of his work on Belgium, is exhibited at Le Botanique in Brussels.

2013 He takes part in the collective project *Transition, paysages d'une société*, in which French and South African photographers capture images of South Africa. This work is exhibited at the Rencontres de la Photographie d'Arles in the same year.

2014 He is now represented by Gallery
Fifty One in Antwerp.
He shoots two ad campaigns for Hermès,
one in Miami for the Spring–Summer
collection, the other in Venice for
the Autumn–Winter collection.

2015 The first retrospective of his work
is held at the Maison Européenne de la
Photographie in Paris.

2018 The retrospective of his work is shown
at FOMU in Antwerp.
Release of Gerrit Messiaen's film *Harry
Gruyaert, photographe*.

2020 He becomes interested in photographic
films and produces video montages
based on several of his series (Belgium,
Morocco, Ireland, Moscow, India). He begins
collaborating with director Valéry Faidherbe
and composer Tuur Florizoone.
A second retrospective of his work is held
at the Hôtel des Arts, Toulon.

2022 He exhibits *Self 07*, a series of
photographs shot for Yves Saint Laurent,
at the Palais Royal in Paris.
His exhibition *Between Worlds* at Gallery
Fifty One in Antwerp is accompanied by
a book of the same name.
Asked to take part in a major photography
project by the Bibliothèque Nationale de
France, he creates a photographic portrait
of the city of Marseille by following the
routes of its three tramlines.

Selected Bibliography

Monographs

1986 *Lumières Blanches*, text by Alain Macaire and Richard Nonas, trans. Brice Matthieussent, Centre National de la Photographie, Paris

1990 *Morocco*, Schirmer/Mosel, Munich

1996 *Dijon vu par Harry Gruyaert*, Mairie de Dijon, Dijon

2000 *Made in Belgium*, text by Hugo Claus, Delpire, Paris

2003 *Rivages*, text byCharles-Arthur Boyer, Textuel, Paris. New ed.: 2008, 2018, Textuel, Paris
Harry Gruyaert, Hachette, 'Les grands photographes de Magnum Photos', Paris

2006 *Harry Gruyaert: Photo Poche*, Actes Sud, Arles

2007 *TV Shots*, text by Jean-Philippe Toussaint, Steidl, Göttingen

2010 *Moscou*, Be-Pôles, Paris

2012 *Roots*, text by Dimitri Verhulst, trans. Alain van Crugsten and Brian Doyle, Xavier Barral, Paris. New ed.: 2018, Xavier Barral, Paris

2013 *Maroc*, text by Brice Matthieussent, Textuel, Paris

2015 *Harry Gruyaert*, text by François Hébel and Richard Nonas, Textuel, Paris; Thames & Hudson, London

2017 *East/West*, text by David Campany, Textuel, Paris; Thames & Hudson, London
It's not about cars, Fifty One, Antwerp

2019 *Last Call*, Textuel, Paris; Thames & Hudson, London
Edges, text by Richard Nonas, Thames & Hudson, London

2020 *Irish Summers*, Fifty One, Antwerp
India, text by Jean-Claude Carrière, Atelier EXB, Paris; Thames & Hudson, London

2022 *Between Worlds*, Atelier EXB, Paris; Thames & Hudson, London

Other publications

1980 *Camera Belgica*, Europalia 80, Brussels
First International Triennial of Photography, Palais des Beaux-Arts, Charleroi

1986 *On the Line: The New Color Photojournalism*, ed. Adam D. Weinberg, Walker Art Center, Minneapolis
The Most Beautiful Place in the World: Impressions of Ten Master Photographers, ed. Jay Maisel, Friendly Press, New York

1988 *Regards d'acier*, ed. Sollac Dunkerque, Centre National de la Photographie, Paris

1989 *Magnum. 50 ans de photographie*, Nathan Images, Paris

1991 *À l'est de Magnum*, Arthaud, Paris

1992 *Département Somme. Regards de photographes*, Trois Cailloux, Amiens
Flesh and Blood: Photographers' Images of Their Own Families, ed. Ethan Hoffmann, Picture Project, New York

1993 *Pour une histoire de la photographie en Belgique*, ed. Georges Verchaval, Musée de la Photographie, Charleroi

1994 *Magnum Cinema*, ed. Alain Bergala, Cahiers du Cinéma/Paris Audiovisuel, Paris; Phaidon, London
A due minuti dal mondo. Storie di uomini e di terre nelle fotografie di dieci grandi autori, Federico Motta, Milan

1996 *Tokyo Today*, ed. Robert Delpire, EU Japan Fest Committee, Tokyo

1998 *Tati 50 x 50*, ed. Fabien Ouaki, Steidl, Göttingen

2000 *I tempi di Roma. Un cantiere fotografico*, Adam Biro, Paris

2002 *Jours de fret*, with Jean Gaumy, Textuel, Paris
Best Regards. Collection NSM Vie-ABN Amro, eds. Elisabeth Nora and Brigitte Ollier, Éditions du Regard, Paris

2003 *New Yorkers As Seen by Magnum Photographers*, ed. Max Kozloff, powerHouse Books, New York

Magnum Degrees, ed. Michael Ignatieff,
Phaidon, London

2004 *La France. Picardie Nord-Pas-de-Calais*,
National Geographic, Gennevilliers
Photographies contemporaines, Groupe
Lhoist, Limelette

2005 *Family: Photographers Photograph
Their Family*, ed. Sophie Spencer-Wood,
Phaidon, London
Magnum Ireland, eds. Anthony Cronin and
Brigitte Lardinois, Thames & Hudson, London

2007 *India Now*, ed. Alain Willaume,
Textuel, Paris
*L'image d'après. Le cinéma dans l'imaginaire
de la photographie*, La Cinémathèque
Française, Paris; Steidl, Göttingen

2009 *Marruecos*, Almuzara, Seville

2011 *Türkiye'de Zaman. Time in Turkey*,
Zaman, Istanbul
En marge. Photographie documentaire belge,
Lannoo, Tielt
*L'Italia e gli Italiani nell'obiettivo dei fotografi
Magnum*, Silvana Editoriale, Milan

2012 *Cartier-Bresson: A Question of Colour*,
Positive View Foundation, London
State of the Art Photography, Feymedia,
Düsseldorf

2013 *Transition, paysages d'une société*,
Xavier Barral, Paris
Grenzgänge Magnum. Trans-Territories,
Kehrer, Heidelberg
*Planche(s) Contact. Festival de photographie
de Deauville*, Filigranes, Trézélan

Cairopolis, Snoeck, Ghent
Le Regardeur. La collection Neuflize Vie,
Xavier Barral, Paris
*Foto/Industria. Bologna Biennale 01 Impresa,
Lavoro*, MAST, Bologna

2015 *Belga cult*, Lannoo, Tielt

2016 *Magnum Cycling*, ed. Guy Andrews,
Thames & Hudson, London
*Transiciones. Diez años que trastornaron
Europa*, La Fábrica, Madrid; Toluca, Paris

2021 *Creatives on Creativity*, ed. Steve
Broumers, Luster, Antwerp

Films

2018 *Harry Gruyaert, photographe*,
directed by Gerrit Messiaen, 70 min.

2019 *Irish Summers,* Harry Gruyaert and
Gallery Fifty One, 8 min.

2021 *Morocco*, Harry Gruyaert and Gallery
Fifty One, 18:35 min.
On the Road / L.A to Las Vegas, Harry
Gruyaert and Gallery Fifty One, 6:36 min.
Made in Belgium, Harry Gruyaert and
Gallery Fifty One, 12:37 min.

2022 *Moscow 1989–2009*, 11:48 min.
India, 14:13 min.
Tokyo, 13:33 min.

Radio programmes

2019 Interview with Marie Richeux, *Par les
temps qui courent*, France Culture, 58 min.

2020 Interview with Arnaud Laporte, *Affaires
culturelles*, France Culture, 56 min.

Selected Exhibitions

1974–1976 *TV Shots*, Galerie Delpire, Paris (with Charles Goossens); Palais des Beaux-Arts, Brussels; International Center of Photography, New York

1978–1980 *Morocco*, Galerie Delpire, Paris; Centre Kodak, Paris; Internationaal Cultureel Centrum, Antwerp; Palais des Beaux-Arts, Brussels; Institut Français, Stockholm

1980–1981 *Made in Belgium*, Palais des Beaux-Arts, Brussels; Galerie Delpire, Paris

1986 *Lumières blanches*, Centre National de la Photographie, Paris

1990 *Harry Gruyaert Fotografías*, Canal de Isabel II, Madrid

1995 *Morocco*, touring exhibition at Moroccan branches of the Institut Français

1997 *Morocco*, Andersen Consulting, Paris

1998 *White Lights/Lumières blanches*, FotoFest, Houston; Galerie Mistral, Montreal

1999 *Morocco*, Laumont Edition Gallery, New York

1999–2000 *Made in Belgium*, Fnac, Brussels; FOMU, Antwerp

2002 *Morocco*, Fundación Carlos de Amberes, Madrid; then touring Spain

2004 *Rivages*, Galerie Saints-Pères, Paris; Rencontres Internationales de la Photographie, Arles

2006 *Morocco*, Galerie Leica, Frankfurt
Rivages, Fundación Caixa Galicia, Lugo/Vigo

2007 *Hommage à Antonioni*, La Cinémathèque Française, Paris

2007–2008 *TV Shots*, Phillips de Pury Gallery, New York & Cologne; Passage du Désir, Paris

2008 *Rivages*, Le Bon Marché, Paris

2009 *Une prétendue réalité*, Magnum Gallery, Paris
TV Shots, Museum für Gestaltung, Zurich
Marruecos, Fundacíon Tres Culturas, Seville

2010 *Moscow 1989–2000*, Glaz Gallery, Moscow; Galerie Philippe Chaume, Paris

2011 *De-ci de-là*, Box Galerie, Brussels
Moscow Photobiennale, Moscow House of Photography, Moscow
Rivages, Galerie du Faouëdic, Lorient
In the Margin, Museum Dr. Guislain, Ghent

2012 *Roots*, Le Botanique, Brussels
Cartier-Bresson. A Question of Colour, Somerset House, London
Moscow 1989–2009, The Manege, Moscow

2013 *Maroc*, Galerie Forêt Verte, Paris
Roots, Magnum Gallery, Paris
Planche(s) Contact, Festival de Photographie de Deauville, Deauville
Raw Materials, *Foto/Industria*, Pinacoteca Nazionale, Bologna

2014 *Hommage à Antonioni*, Galerie Cinéma, Paris

2015 *Harry Gruyaert*, Maison Européenne de la Photographie, Paris

2016 *Hommage à Antonioni*, Librairie Maupetit, Marseille

2017 *Western & Eastern Light*, Michael Hoppen Gallery, London

2018 *Rivages*, Galerie Yvon Lambert, Paris
Roots, Gallery Fifty One, Antwerp
Harry Gruyaert. Retrospective, FOMU, Antwerp
It's not about cars, Gallery Fifty One, Antwerp

2019 *Rivages*, Base Sous Marine, Bordeaux
Bordeaux vu par Harry Gruyaert, Galerie Arrêt sur l'Image, Bordeaux
Harry Gruyaert, Hôtel des Arts, Toulon

2020 *Harry Gruyaert*, Howard Greenberg Gallery, New York
Harry Gruyaert. Retrospective, Museum Helmond, Helmond

2022 *Between Worlds*, Gallery Fifty One, Antwerp

The Photofile series is the original English-language edition of the Photo Poche collection. It was first published between 1986 and 1992 by the Centre National de la Photographie, Paris, with the support of the French Ministry of Culture. Robert Delpire (1926–2017) was the creator of the series and its managing editor until 2017.

General editor: Géraldine Lay

Series design by Matthew Young

Translated from the French

First published in the United Kingdom in 2023 by
Thames & Hudson Ltd, 181A High Holborn, London WC1V 7QX

First published in the United States of America in 2023 by
Thames & Hudson Inc., 500 Fifth Avenue, New York, New York 10110

Reprinted in 2024

British Library Cataloguing-in-Publication Data
A catalogue record for this book is available from the British Library

Library of Congress Control Number 2022946950

ISBN 978-0-500-29730-8

Printed and bound in Italy

Be the first to know about our new releases,
exclusive content and author events by visiting
thamesandhudson.com
thamesandhudsonusa.com
thamesandhudson.com.au